KILLER IN THE FAMILY

ALSO BY MELISSA G. MOORE AND MICHELE MATRISCIANI

Shattered Silence: The Untold Story of a Serial Killer's Daughter

WHOLE: How I Learned to Fill the Fragments of My Life with Forgiveness, Hope, Strength, and Creativity

Released: Conversations on the Eve of Freedom with Gypsy-Rose Blanchard

My Time to Stand: A Memoir (by Gypsy-Rose Blanchard with Melissa G. Moore and Michele Matrisciani)

KILLER IN THE FAMILY

THE HIDDEN COSTS OF LOVING SOMEONE THE WORLD HATES

MELISSA G. MOORE AND

MICHELE MATRISCIANI

BENBELLA

BenBella Books, Inc.
Dallas, TX

DISCLAIMER: This book draws on Melissa Moore's personal recollections, interviews with family members of victims and offenders, deposition transcripts, court records, and other publicly available documents and statements. To protect privacy and safety, certain names, identifying details, and personal characteristics have been changed or omitted. In some instances, quoted dialogue has been lightly edited for readability, including the removal of stutters, verbal tics, and repeated words. While the author has made reasonable efforts to ensure accuracy, some conversations and events are paraphrased or reconstructed from memory or reflect the subjective impressions and recollections of the family members interviewed for this book.

BENBELLA

BenBella Books, Inc.
8080 N. Central Expressway
Suite 1700
Dallas, TX 75206
benbellabooks.com
Send feedback to feedback@benbellabooks.com

BenBella is a federally registered trademark.

Printed in the United States of America
10 9 8 7 6 5 4 3 2 1

Library of Congress Control Number: 2026021898
ISBN 9781637749586 (trade paperback)
ISBN 9781637749593 (electronic)

Editing by Scott Calamar
Copyediting by Elizabeth Degenhard
Proofreading by Rebecca Maines
Text design and composition by Aaron Edmiston
Cover design by Kara Klontz
Cover image © Adobe Stock / david (windows) and © iStock / Artem Koviazin (torn paper) and Simon Herrmann (tape)
Printed by Lake Book Manufacturing

For the sons, daughters, mothers, fathers, spouses, and siblings who carry a name that doesn't tell the whole story—the families who never asked to join this "club."

CONTENTS

INTRODUCTION

A NOTE FROM MELISSA

This is not your typical true crime book, though it is a book about many heinous crimes, and it's all true. The best books in this genre give a voice to the people whose voices were stolen. But as the daughter of a serial killer, I can't help but get wrapped up in those *other* stolen lives that the murderer carried away with them: those of his or her family members.

Membership in the club of killer family members is selective and exclusive, and it's sealed with a ritual. The ritual has two parts: experiencing various stages of grief (shock, denial, and bargaining with God to make it all go away being the most prominent and extensive) and the media storm, complete with occasional stalking and explosions of speculation—online, on television, and even in person—that blast the character of the family members who love the killer.

The feelings of family members of perpetrators are routinely discounted, despite their emotional losses as well as the physical absence (by death or incarceration) of someone they once deeply loved, still do, or have learned to hate. Their identity as someone's parent, sibling, spouse, in-law, or child is now ripped from them as the media recasts their character and speculates on what they had to have known or suspected, or in some cases failed to notice.

When a murder is committed, the families of the victim and perpetrator both endure a baptism by fire, and *both* are initiated into the club. They will forever be connected as a kind of kin, though one side is generally greeted with sympathy and the other with unrelenting scorn. Most refuse to see how both sides are joined by a crime, not divided by it.

This paradox is what I wanted to explore in this true crime book with a slightly different angle. I also had a personal reason for doing so: this is the book I promised my mother I would write. Uterine cancer took her swiftly . . . so swiftly that she entered hospice care on a Friday and died the next Sunday. I truly believe there is some sort of energetic connection to her suffering from that sort of female-centric cancer that relates to her many years as a victim of domestic abuse. Her second husband, my stepfather, caused plenty of damage, but by the time my father exited our family, the real damage had been done. After that, my mother was physically and mentally exhausted. She could no longer take care of herself, speak up for herself, or value her own life.

One of the last things my mother said to me on her deathbed was "I'm your dad's last victim . . . it just took longer for him to kill me." In a strange last twist to their tale, she died on my dad's birthday.

I have been advocating for victims of crimes as well as what I call their "secondary victims" for more than a decade now. Through three previously published books, a cable network series, a podcast, and a scripted CBS show about my life, I am committed to giving these secondary victims a chance to have a bigger voice.

When something like this happens to you, you become part of a circus, in which you are the clown. You put on a happy face, your painted smile disguising the humiliation, your act concealing the grief that spills out only when the audience is gone. In a world where the happy family is worn like a costume, you never really know if the smiles you see are just a mask hiding the truth.

Once the media starts to tail you, your family and personal pain are exploited as clickbait. My work in the media is all about doing the opposite.

I want to help people in our small club, which we never wanted to be in, to feel safe enough to share, because for so many years, I felt unsafe and wanted only to hide. This book is their chance to tell their own stories. My own mother never told hers, not until she was letting go of the life that had blindsided her. She had been fooled by the happy face worn by her husband (by both of them, frankly), a disguise so many other families tragically learned to recognize, only after it was too late. This is the book I promised her I would write as she lay dying.

My interviews with the contributors in this book became tearful conversations, mutual confessions, a reciprocation of vulnerability, and a shared experience of the torment of not being able to shut off your love for someone most people believe does not deserve it. Some of our talks were solicited by a family member. I'm pretty easy to find, and it isn't uncommon for people who are thrust into this awful club of having a killer in the family to share with me, looking to relate and glean understanding and hope. Other interviewees I sought out because I wanted to explore as many different relational dynamics as possible—from parent and child to sibling and spouse to grandchild and in-law. What if the son you took to Little League grew up to kill your grandchildren? What if your nana who served you cookies also served time for dismembering her mother? What if the father who called you "princess" and kissed your forehead at bedtime was a serial killer? It might not be common to have a killer in the family, but once we recognize that such families, too, live the same ordinary moments we do, the line dividing us gives way to our shared humanity.

Our talks uncovered debilitating trauma that forever ruined the lives of those family members. When their loved ones were locked away, it left them with the residue of guilt that, somehow, they should have known or seen beforehand what would happen; that if they had done something different, lives would have been saved.

Could have, would have, should have: the burden is lifelong. Family members will continually question the validity of all their relationships and second-guess motives and their own judgment. In the particular hell where parents of murderers dwell, they wonder whether they were somehow the devil's gateway to Earth.

The mother of Ted Kaczynski, the Unabomber, was reported as saying to the widow of one of her son's victims, "I wish he had killed me instead of your husband." This sentiment is a thread that connects each and every person included in this book. If they could undo it all, they would, even at their own expense.

This book is an outgrowth of my lifelong unexpected mission: to give those who have been demonized the opportunity to verbalize their feelings, and hopefully to grieve in solidarity with the families of victims instead of in the lone shadow of shame.

CASE #1

KEITH JESPERSON, THE "HAPPY FACE SERIAL KILLER"

THE CRIME

Washington state resident Keith Hunter Jesperson, who stood an imposing six feet six inches tall and weighed around 250 pounds, worked mainly as a long- and short-haul truck driver, a job that took him to far-flung states and facilitated the serial murdering of women. His first victim, Taunja Bennett, was strangled (his preferred method of killing) and her body discovered in 1990; over the next five years seven more women's bodies were discovered. Annoyed at the press attention focused on other suspects, for several years Jesperson taunted the media and law enforcement with handwritten confession letters signed with a smiley face, causing a journalist at Portland's *Oregonian* to dub him the "Happy Face Killer."

And there were other suspects: in an odd red herring, fifty-seven-year-old Laverne Pavlinac implicated her live-in boyfriend, John Sosnovske, in Bennett's rape and murder. Pavlinac's detailed narrative painted a grim picture of Sosnovske coercing her to participate in Bennett's vicious attack and the disposal of her body. Pavlinac and Sosnovske were apprehended on March 5, 1990, and convicted of the murder on February 8, 1991. However, Pavlinac later admitted to fabricating her confession. She had crafted a false narrative from information she had gleaned from newspaper accounts to escape her abusive relationship with Sosnovske, inadvertently incriminating herself as an accomplice.

When Keith Jesperson was questioned in 1995 after a recent girlfriend was found murdered, he realized he would soon be apprehended; he wrote a letter to his brother detailing the murders of eight women in the past five years. After two failed suicide attempts, he turned himself in to law enforcement and confessed to the murder of his former girlfriend . . . and a host of others: more than a hundred. There was definitive proof for one: police had saved the stamp from a Happy Face Killer letter sent to journalist Phil Stanford in 1994; DNA in the saliva was a match for the DNA found on Taunja Bennett's body.

Jesperson was sentenced to life in prison for the murder of his former girlfriend by a Washington Superior Court judge in 1995. Shortly thereafter, he was given two additional life sentences for the earlier murders of his two Oregon victims. In 1998, a Wyoming judge sentenced him to yet another life term, to run concurrent with his three previous life sentences, virtually assuring he would die in prison.

THE VICTIMS

The "Happy Face" serial killer claimed the lives of eight known victims:

Taunja Bennett (1990): Strangled to death, her body discovered near the town of Ferndale, Washington.

Jane Doe (1992): An unidentified woman Jesperson called "Claudia," found raped and murdered around Blythe, California.

Cynthia Lyn Rose (1992): Strangled body found in Turlock, California.

Laurie Ann Pentland (1992): Strangled near Salem, Oregon.

Patricia Skiple (1993): Killed in Santa Nella, California. Thanks to the Jane Doe Project, Skiple is no longer a Jane Doe.

Angela Subrize (1993): Body discovered near Crestview, Florida.

Suzanne Kjellenberg (1994): Another Jane Doe until October of 2023. DNA testing confirmed the identity of the woman Jesperson recalled only as "Susan" or "Suzette," whose body was found in Crestview, Florida.

Julie Ann Winningham (1995): A former girlfriend of Jesperson's and the only victim to have a personal relationship with him, she was strangled to death and her nude body tossed over an embankment alongside State Highway 14 in Clark County.

Daun Richert-Slagle (1990): A twenty-one-year-old mother of three who is the only known victim to survive an attack. While Daun filed a police report at the time, claiming Jesperson had tried to strangle her in his car, the case was deemed a "he-said, she-said" after detectives brought Jesperson in for questioning. He was released due to lack of evidence to link him to the allegation and roamed free for five more years.

While Jesperson has claimed to have killed as many as 160 people, only these eight murders have been conclusively confirmed.

TODAY

Jesperson has been behind bars at the Oregon State Penitentiary in Salem since 1995 and maintains regular contact with the media. His story about the number of his victims continues to change; the true extent of his crimes will remain a mystery.

THE MEDIA

The Oregonian, Portland, Oregon. Journalist Phil Stanford dubbed Jesperson the "Happy Face Killer" and covered the case extensively. His 2021 exposé, "The Happy Face Murders: Death in the Pacific Northwest," served as a turning point in the investigation of the Pavlinac/Sosnovske false confessions and garnered national attention. (Pavlinac and Sosnovske were released from prison after serving four years.)

I: The Creation of a Serial Killer (2002). Book by Jack Olsen. Drawing heavily on diaries, letters, and personal interviews with Jesperson, this bestseller became a classic in the true crime genre.

Dark Minds (2012). True crime TV series with author M. William Phelps and criminal profiler John Kelly. Jesperson speaks (voice masked) and is credited as "Serial Murder Consultant."

Dangerous Ground: My Friendship with a Serial Killer (2017). Book by true crime journalist M. William Phelps.

Happy Face Killer (2014). Lifetime television movie starring David Arquette as Keith Jesperson.

Happy Face (2025). CBS-scripted drama airing on Paramount+ starring Dennis Quaid as Keith Jesperson and Annaleigh Ashford as Melissa Reed [Melissa Moore's fictionalized character].

LEFT BEHIND

Daughter Melissa G. Moore and her sister and brother; life changed forever in March 1995.

CHAPTER 1

WHEN A DAUGHTER HAS A KILLER DAD

LEFT BEHIND: DAUGHTER MELISSA G. MOORE

The wound is the place the light enters you.

—Rumi

When I turned in the first draft of this manuscript, I was proud of the roster of participants I had lined up. Each family listed in the table of contents represented years of trust-building, emotional bonding, and raw, vulnerable truth. My new book profiled families like ours—left shell-shocked, grappling, and silenced by shame. I was proud of how that work was reflected in the manuscript. I hit send with a feeling of satisfaction at a job well done.

The very next afternoon my email pinged on my phone as I was working.

"Where's *your* story?" My collaborator, Michele, got right to the point.

The three little words startled me; my cheeks got hot.

"One would think readers would want to begin with your story about having the Happy Face Killer as a father."

One would think. Except I hadn't. The entire premise of this book is to help families let go of the stigma and talk about their struggles, and yet I had completely written mine out.

Michele's email went on, "The crimes your father committed, and the havoc they wreaked on your life, cannot be ignored in the context of the book's themes."

Dammit. I was afraid she'd say that.

For many people, finding the words (at least finding the right words) doesn't always come naturally. Thanks to books by women about women, from *Jane Eyre* to *Little Women,* I was in love with words from a young age, but our family dynamic was not to use them. I internalized very early on that we didn't talk about Dad's infidelities, my parents' divorce, and our constant financial struggles.

We certainly never spoke about the eight women my father confessed to raping, murdering, and abandoning in the woods up and down the Pacific coast. On the night everything changed I was lying on my cot in the basement of my grandmother's house in Spokane, dreaming of a room of my own. The homes in my grandmother's neighborhood had originally been built for military families who worked at nearby Fairchild Air Force Base. Every modest dwelling on the street was the same, one small cookie-cutter place after another. My grandmother's single-story home was no more than 1,000 square feet. My grandmother Delores, my uncle Steve, and my uncle Charles lived upstairs.

The rest of us lived downstairs. Down a set of rough-painted gray wooden stairs—no backing—led to one large square cement basement.

A wall in one corner featured a two-foot by four-foot recessed window that let in a bit of infrequent light. A washer and dryer sat in another corner, next to support beams encased in cement that held up the house. Cheap paneling formed a partially finished wall in another corner, which did feature a hinged door. That was my brother's "room," partitioned off for a bit of privacy.

My sister slept on a twin-size mattress laid directly on the cement floor. A home canning operation took up another corner, with a couple of pull strings dangling from overhead light bulbs above it; I had placed a cot there and stacked up some shoeboxes to serve as my drawers. There was another tiny window in that corner, which is why I chose it.

My mom and stepdad had partitioned off the far back area with more fake wood paneling and another hinged door. Their queen-size mattress on a bare metal frame sat atop a piece of red remnant carpeting. They did have a battered old dresser there for their clothing, and a wooden crib for my new half brother Jonathan. Our cat, Tabitha, lived with us in the basement—she mostly stayed in Mom's room.

I had fallen into a sound sleep when a light appeared at the top of the stairs, and I heard my mother coming. "Kids?" she called, then again, a little louder. "Kids? I have something to tell you all."

My brother Jason emerged from his corner, walked to the lighted stairway, and looked up at Mom, head cocked. I sat up in my cot, alarmed. My stomach was tight; I felt the hair on the back of my neck rising. Something was very wrong.

Mom got halfway down and looked at her three wide-eyed kids. "Your dad's in jail," she said flatly, then turned around to head back upstairs.

"Mom, wait!" my brother Jason cried. She halted, her back to us, nearly to the door at the top of the stairs. "Dad's in jail? Why, what for?"

"For murder," she said. Then she took the last couple of steps up, exited the basement, and shut the door firmly behind her. That was all she had to say about that. We knew better than to ask for details. We would never dream of pressing her; that was not our way.

In shock, we retreated to our separate areas as my little sister Carrie cried disconsolately. Somehow, we slept that night, and in the morning we headed off to school as usual, without another word spoken about my father. After school, in the downtown Spokane library, I found an article in a Vancouver newspaper reporting that my father had confessed to the murder of his former girlfriend, Julie Winningham, and was currently being held in Clark County Jail. I knew Julie . . . slim with feathered honey-blonde hair. The last time I'd seen my dad he had said they were getting engaged, and he spun me a pretty picture of a new home he would build on some land he planned to buy in coastal Astoria, where we'd all live together as a family. And now Julie's nude, strangled body had been found and my dad was the cause?

Due to our deeply ingrained pattern of swallowing our words along with our feelings, I had never burdened my mother by telling her about my father's questionable behavior when we spent time together, which included his sexually explicit conversations with me, the perverted gestures he made to diner waitresses, and the way he'd describe the details of his sexual conquests, like we were barroom buddies comparing bedpost notches over Coors Light. He had no problem telling me, his teenage daughter, that their divorce was partly because my mother "wasn't good in bed."

He constantly manipulated all three of us kids, guilt-tripping us by constantly moaning to us about how poor he was because he had to pay child support. Once he had even gone so far as to tell us he wanted to go to jail, since prisoners were relieved of paying child support. Well, I guess he'd gotten that wish.

As unbelievable as this news was, I could not have fathomed that the news of Julie's murder was only the tip of the iceberg.

Just thinking back on those days in my life brought up such turmoil in me. I was no longer that sad, scared, fifteen-year-old girl; I'd come a long way since then. The reason for my resistance to being in my own book was the dreaded thought of telling my story yet again, the same way I'd always told it. How I am the daughter of a serial killer, how I lived in shame, how I tried to do penance for my father by meeting the family members of his victims. But in the nearly thirty years since that time, the story had continued and evolved.

I think there are many reasons we feel compelled to tell our stories. The first is to make sense of what happened to ourselves. The second is to share the story with others, as I had been doing for years. I wanted to turn my internal growth outward and hoped to inspire others to own their own stories and face the truth of their pain. As I grappled with what to do about my own chapter, I realized there was a third reason: to affirm one's present life. To tell the story not from the perspective of the story's origin but from the place where it finally comes to an end, so that a new story can begin. I decided I would not tell the story yet again of being the daughter of the Happy Face Killer, but the story of how I became Melissa Moore.

HOW I BECAME MELISSA MOORE

It was a very different time, media-wise, back in the 1990s. Most Americans got all their news from their local paper or evening news. I lived in Spokane, and my father's major murder trials were held in Oregon, so our family was largely spared from being harassed. Reporters weren't following me home from school like they would today. Back then, local news stayed local, and Washington and Oregon were not usually hotbeds of big breaking news. The parents of some of my friends did see a broadcast about Julie's murder and were a little alarmed. They got together with other parents and had a discussion. The upshot was that distance should be put between their kids and me—immediately.

This is certainly understandable, given that they had unwittingly exposed their child to a serial killer. As an adult and parent, I now understand that reaction, but I was very hurt by this guilt by association at that age. I couldn't understand the sudden pulling away of my friends and the chill from their parents, who had always liked me. I had plenty of trauma to deal with already; I forged on. I had no idea how lucky I was to remain relatively unscathed by the media.

My father, on the other hand, was never shy, and he certainly courted media attention after his arrest. This led the reigning dean of true crime, author Jack Olsen, to write a book about him. I had just graduated from high school when the hardcover came out, and it got a lot of play locally, but I was completely focused on cosmetology school and getting ahead. I had my head down, blinders on, working hard at school, 100 percent driven to getting myself *out*. I knew that Olsen had interviewed my grandfather, Les, and even dropped a free copy of the book at our house; but I had not read it. I had no desire.

A couple of years later, my longtime boyfriend Sam and I walked into a Barnes & Noble only to be confronted with a large pop-up stand featuring stacks of *I: The Creation of a Serial Killer* in a new paperback edition. It was shocking to see a familiar personal photograph of my smiling dad on the cover and blown up to movie-poster size as part of the cardboard display. Sam couldn't believe it; he picked up a copy and examined it closely. All I could say was "That's my dad." It was a surreal, other-worldly feeling as curious shoppers buzzed around us. Just walking into a bookstore, of all places, and there he was, in my face, larger than life.

I did not buy the paperback that day, but at some point I decided to read the book. I started, but I quickly stopped. It was beyond painful to read. Jack Olsen had captured my father's voice so well that I could hear him in my head, talking to me. It was spooky . . . and so incredibly shocking. I could not get past the part where my dad described Taunja Bennett, his first victim, because she looked so much like my mom. Nor could I stomach the graphic descriptions of her murder, not to mention the discussions of his sex life with my mom, disturbing in an entirely different way. To this day, I have never finished the book. After my one attempt to actually read it, I returned to trying to make a new life for myself . . . which I was doing step by painful step.

My father had given me one decent piece of advice: he told me to change my last name, which I did after I married Sam. As Melissa Moore I became a mom at the young age of twenty-one, having first my daughter, Aspen, and three years later my son, Jake. My days were pretty typical, filled with chaperoning field trips, packing lunches, and nursing fevers. Ten years after my father's conviction, I'd moved away to Texas, worked in a salon, then completely assumed my new identity as a stay-at-home mom running a small daycare operation out of my home. It had become a habit to make myself smaller, to be quiet and private and unassuming in my low-key life.

One night in 2000 as I prepared dinner, I heard a newscaster discussing the trial of Robert Lee Yates. This was a case I'd followed for obvious reasons. Yates was a serial killer from Washington state. He, too, had a wife and family who'd been thunderstruck by the murders Yates had committed as the Grocery Bag Killer. This was a big, big story in Spokane . . . and footage of his family made it all the way to Texas television.

I was struck by the expressions on the faces of Yates's wife and children. His daughters were close to my age, and I remember recognizing the blankness in their eyes, thinking they were probably among the few people on Earth who could understand me. It was like lightning struck and zapped me with the electrifying realization that I wasn't alone. I wanted to call up the family immediately and tell them I knew exactly how they felt. But I had no way of reaching out other than through a journalist, and I wasn't about to expose myself or my family history. I was still quite anonymous, and grateful for my quiet life.

Shortly afterward, my then six-year-old daughter came home from school, curious about her family tree. How could she not be? Her Crayola-colored tree was so lopsided. I had never told her a thing about her maternal grandfather. We lived quite near my husband's family, and the kids enjoyed a great relationship with one set of grandparents—that was good enough for me.

"Mommy, everybody has a daddy, where's yours?" she asked, looking up at me with no doubt that I would tell her the truth.

Looking down at her inquisitive face, I could not bear to tell her that my daddy was a serial killer serving three life sentences in the Oregon State Penitentiary. All I could think to say in response was "He lives in Salem," which was barely half a truth. I had run from the truth for as long as I could remember, but there's nothing like a six-year-old to stop you dead in your tracks and make you question your life choices. I quickly changed the subject, but I was left to wonder how I could ever tell her everything. I hated the idea that she might come to think evil coursed through her veins. It was my own never-ending pain and shame, and the fear of instilling both in my child, that sent me in search of help.

As a Texas transplant, I had become familiar with Dr. Phil, the straight-talking psychologist whose appearance on *The Oprah Winfrey Show* eventually led to hosting his own popular daytime show, *Dr. Phil.* I did not want my father's notoriety as a serial killer to harm my children's lives. I knew I needed real help, and I sent an email humbly asking for it. The very next day the show reached out, and we began a correspondence. At the producers' request, I began filming homemade video diaries about my life and questions for Dr. Phil. Eventually I was invited to be a part of his Get Real Retreat along with thirteen other participants from all sorts of backgrounds. On Father's Day weekend in 2008 I boarded a plane for Los Angeles to enter an intensive program to be filmed to air on the show.

A union makeup artist worked on the Dr. Phil set, and as soon as I arrived I realized that every day I would have a professional applying my makeup. How I loved that part of the experience . . . I was completely dazzled by this woman. It was my secret ambition to go to Hollywood and work as a makeup artist; suddenly here I was sitting in a chair, being tended to by a woman who was living the dream. This was a life I couldn't have imagined at the time—living in LA? Working in television? I did not know anybody who had such a glamorous job.

The retreat was filmed long before the reality TV show craze; none of the participants were seeking fame. Believe me, no one there wanted to be famous—we were all so very vulnerable. There were fourteen men and women at our retreat; it was a very intense group. The premise was that each person was "stuck" in some way in their life and needed to make a massive change. One woman, also from Texas, had some issues with racism, due to a bad experience with a Black man. A man was suffering from some sort of sexual addiction, stemming from his sexually abusive childhood. Another girl's father had committed suicide and she couldn't get past it; another woman was a Canadian sex worker trying to leave it behind; another woman's husband had assaulted her.

Every single person on that show was seeking some professional guidance on how to learn to live in a different way; their motives were pure. We were all throwing ourselves at Dr. Phil, hoping he would be the Wizard of Oz and lead us to our very own Yellow Brick Roads.

The stories people told ran the full gamut of dysfunction. Even so, when I stepped forward to speak, the feeling in the room instantly changed. When I started to share who my father was, describe the crimes he had committed, and how I felt about this legacy, people became visibly uncomfortable. It was almost as if they felt their problems weren't so bad after all after hearing this. That's how I felt, anyway. I didn't like this feeling; I would never want someone not to share their problems with me because, next to mine, they seem like small potatoes. One thing I knew for sure: there is no hierarchy of pain; it is the great equalizer. My cross to bear was trying to navigate life and parenthood as the daughter of a serial killer.

"You got a shitty deal," Dr. Phil told me, and he advised that I must learn to separate my father's crimes from my own life, as they were not mine and I had no reason to be ashamed. I had been carrying a heavy load of fear and guilt for years; it was time to lay it down. Simple, but powerful. My new friends received equally no-nonsense advice. And we worked on it. As we dispersed back to our homes after filming, we all had some new coping tools. And then it was showtime.

Dr. Phil was a popular national daytime show, so the whole country was about to learn who I was. I had never seen another person with a background like mine successfully tell their story or come off in any kind of positive light. The family member of a perpetrator coming forward of their own free will and telling their story was quite a new thing at the time. Family members of killers tended to be lambasted in the press, ostracized in their communities, and generally persecuted. I was terrified when it was time for that show to air. I had been so sheltered, spared a media storm, and now I was turning that bright light on myself, inviting scrutiny and judgment. I had so many worries: I was afraid my husband might lose his job. I was afraid I would lose clients at my home-based childcare business. Both were very real possibilities.

The three-episode "Retreat" show was a ratings hit. I was featured quite prominently throughout. It was strange to see myself on television. I was not looking my best, as anxiety had gotten the best of me that week; I looked bloated and uncomfortable onscreen. And all anonymity was forever gone. However, none of the dire consequences I feared actually came to pass. What happened instead was that people I associated with—neighbors, casual friends, other parents from my kids' school—started approaching me. Many opened along the lines of "You're so brave for coming forward," and then followed up with the most intimate details of their lives. For example, *My brother was a pedophile.* I wasn't prepared for revelations like that!

It felt as though some floodgates had opened. Because they had seen me share my story on television, people now, unprompted, felt free to share their most shameful stories. Not just people I knew—strangers, too, approached me when they recognized me. I was dealing with a minor insurance claim in my kitchen at the time, and the adjuster who came out to assess the damage recognized me from the show and started confiding in me about the sexual abuse she had suffered as a kid. It was mind-blowing. All these people, all these families that looked so perfect on the outside . . . of course, every family has their own private issues, but I truly had no idea of the scope. I had been too lost in my own misery.

I was particularly moved by the many family members who had a killer in their own family and reached out to thank me for sharing my own story. They were eager to share their own troubles. The more I emailed with them, talked to them on the phone, listened to their journeys, met others through them, the more I became convinced that I had done the right thing by coming forward. We were forming a small but intensely healing community. We understood each other like no one else ever could or would.

I was in uncharted territory, and the responsibility I had taken on began to reveal itself slowly, like petals opening. I felt so liberated. Now, I *wanted* to tell my story. Dr. Phil had told me that confronting my denial by articulating the shame and grief that had crippled me all these years would be a positive leap toward healing. I had not gone into much detail about my own childhood on the show, so I decided to write my memoir. It took an entire year to get it down on paper, and I wound up with hundreds of pages in a huge Word document. I had done my best to write it myself, but I had no guidance or other books to look to. Try as I might, I could not find any book by a family member of a killer on the bookshelves. There was simply no roadmap to follow.

I could find plenty of true crime books, so I considered recasting my story as a true crime tale, but that was not the right approach. I hit the wall. I remember going to my room, looking at these messy stacks of typed manuscript pages, and just throwing up my hands. I uttered an out-loud prayer: *I can't do any more, please help me,* I prayed. *I know I need to tell my story, but I don't know how.*

And then, almost as if in answer to my prayer, I found a book by a skinhead-turned-activist named TJ Leyden—a dark topic, not one I would ever be drawn to read about. But the writing was so soft, the storytelling so compelling, that I was drawn in. Bridget was the coauthor's name, and I reached out to her. She said, "Send me the manuscript you have." After reviewing my pages, she said, "Let's start over. From the beginning." Our work together was a truly intense form of therapy that went on for an entire year. There were times I had to shut down and stop, as I didn't want to relive these memories or talk about my childhood anymore. But the book eventually took shape and found a small publisher. The story—*my* story, every painful detail about growing up as the daughter of Keith Jesperson—was going to be out there.

My husband had always been a big cheerleader for my work; he did everything he could to support me. He had been all for me appearing on the Dr. Phil show; he supported all my efforts to birth that book: financially, emotionally, in every way possible. He always believed in my mission. It was amazing to see the galleys (pre-publication advance bound copies) of my very own book. Late that summer my husband became active on Twitter—it had become a thing—where he followed some producers on *The Oprah Winfrey Show*.

I had no idea what an executive producer was at that time, but one tweeted out, "I'm looking for some incredible stories for the next season of the show." My husband tweeted back, "You should read my wife's book, just about to come out—she's the daughter of a serial killer." The producer was intrigued; they exchanged DMs, she requested a galley, and next thing I knew I was on the *Oprah* show during the season premiere week in September 2009. There I was in Chicago, with my mother by my side . . . oh, and Dr. Phil, too—he was there to tout his "discovery." Though not an official Oprah Book Club Selection, she promoted *Shattered Silence* for an entire hour, and it sold many, many copies, a genuine hit. It rocked my world!

If the *Dr. Phil* show hadn't done it, Oprah did . . . it suddenly seemed that the whole world knew who I was now! Journalist Lisa Ling, one of

CNN's special correspondents, reached out to say she wanted me on the show to tell my story, and meanwhile, did I know anybody else with a similar story? I certainly did. I reached out to some of the family members I'd come to know. I only gave out their contact details with their permission, of course, only if they expressed an interest in any media attention. I began to feel that this sort of "matchmaking" was my forte, something that had started so organically.

I was beginning to understand how television production worked. I started to imagine: What would it be like if I had my *own* show where I could tell other people's stories? And then, just like that, a production company reached out to me. "You have such an incredible story! Would you like to bring other people's experiences to the forefront as well?" And that is how the show *Monster in My Family* came to be. Now this was a topic near and dear to my heart. The show connected secondary victims—perpetrators' family members—with family members of the victims so that they could express their remorse and sympathies.

The show covered many prominent true crime cases. The Yates girls—Robert Lee Yates's daughters—made an appearance on *Monster in My Family*, truly a full-circle moment for me. I was so happy to meet them. The show aired for two seasons, and I continued to learn the ins and outs of television production. I was becoming a part of the media world! And making industry connections, which proved to be helpful. The field director had a job interview at Warner Bros. Telepictures, and during the process she told producers that her last job had been in true crime, working with me on *Monster in My Family*. They brought me in and said, "How about being a crime correspondent for us?" I didn't have a clue what that involved, but I said yes, absolutely.

I was not a staffer or official employee on *Crime Watch Daily*; I would be paid for stories I brought to the show. This was easy for me: all I had to do was sort through the hundreds of private emails from families. I contacted a number of them to see if they might want to appear on *Crime Watch Daily;* many did. I traveled the nation meeting all these people and told all kinds of stories. Work was going so well that our family relocated to Los Angeles in 2014. We moved to the suburb of Santa Clarita, and I supported myself as a television professional.

A year into this freelance work, I got an offer to come to New York to tell my own story again on the *Dr. Oz Show.* The show was known for its focus on medical angles: health, wellness, diet and exercise, natural cures . . . but all of a sudden true crime was the hot commodity, and they were considering diving into this new world. One of the producers on staff was persuading Dr. Oz to explore this new topic, so I was booked to tell my story as one of the show's first true crime guests.

The ratings were amazing, which naturally led once again to the question: *Do you have other stories to share?* I started in a freelance position again, being paid for each story I brought to producers. I started what became a very popular show—*True Crime Tuesdays*—and we were off to the races. New producers were being hired on; it became quite a thing. I was soon offered a salaried position.

I worked at *The Dr. Oz Show* for five years, a very happy professional time in my life. Dr. Oz was kind and respectful; he listened to me and gave me plenty of space to do my job. He was naturally inquisitive about each case and genuinely wanted to know details; he appreciated the perspective I could bring to each case. The true crime genre worked well for his show, and I was surrounded by great talent. Ethical, professional, on their own storytelling missions.

I continued to work on myself as well. I read everything I could in the search for understanding of how we process trauma and heal. Then, I was introduced to a woman who would become my true partner in storytelling, a brilliant writer named Michele Matrisciani. As a bestselling acquisitions editor at several publishing houses and an author herself, Michele has access to so many different areas; she opened my eyes to entire new worlds when it came to reframing my life and story. She introduced me to amazing healing, growth, and self-empowerment modalities. We chronicled my journey together in my second book,

WHOLE: How I Learned to Fill the Fragments of My Life with Forgiveness, Hope, Strength, and Creativity, in which we interviewed renowned researchers, doctors, therapists, spiritual healers, even a famous psychic. It was critically acclaimed!

I was beginning to really understand how every facet of this business of telling your story—or someone else's—worked. What it really took to bring a story to print in book form, or on the television airwaves.

Dr. Oz began to consider dabbling in podcasting. Podcasts were the new next big thing at that time, and his producers all thought his content would lend itself well to that format. So, one day Dr. Oz pulled me aside and asked me if he could interview me for a potential podcast . . . of course, I agreed. I told him some stories on our episode, which eventually made its way into a pitch meeting. The media service iHeartRadio offered us both deals (part of my royalties went to Dr. Oz). My humble little podcast was mostly recorded in my dressing room, on the fly. I called it *Happy Face Presents: Two Face* and interviewed a number of fascinating guests.

The move to California had been a great success, but by 2018, my marriage was dying. Sam and I separated but maintained one main house for the kids' stability, where we took turns staying. My schedule could not have been better for a working mother—the show went on hiatus every summer, giving me three months off. This was ideal for raising my kids. Despite the sadness that came when Sam and I divorced, working there was a great time in my life, very fulfilling. And thanks to the work I'd been doing for years, I was confident I could carry on by myself.

And then, my life changed like everyone else in the country's. The COVID-19 pandemic put an end to my job; it shut down the entire city of New York where Dr. Oz was based. Everything turned to Zoom—in my last year on the show that was the only way I could conduct interviews. Telling other people's stories had become how I made my own living. Now, I couldn't do that so easily. Suddenly, I was on unemployment. It was a very lean time. I eked out a living helping people pitch their stories to television executives and got some credits. A small Paycheck Protection Program (PPP) loan to my tiny independent production company was all that kept me afloat as I got serious about chasing two compelling stories I had long been personally drawn to.

One was Gypsy-Rose Blanchard, the young woman whose boyfriend had killed her mother in Missouri after Gypsy had suffered years of abuse at her mother's hands. I'd been thinking of Gypsy for seven years, ever since I'd gone to see her in a Missouri prison. The second was a story about Nicole Brown Simpson. I'd long had a strong interest in the crime of the century, given that I spent years watching my mom stay for much too long in an abusive, violent relationship.

An old colleague from *Monster in My Family* called me and said she had a new position in TV development . . . and if I had any documentaries to pitch, she was all ears. I pitched her these two cases that were near and dear to my heart, and both eventually went into production. *Gypsy-Rose Blanchard: Prison Confessions* aired to really huge numbers. The story that I had long wanted to do with Nicole Brown's sisters—Denise, Dominique, and Tanya—came out in June 2024, on the thirtieth anniversary of their sister's murder. Michele and I teamed up again to bring Gypsy-Rose Blanchard's story to ebook form in 2024 and then collaborated with Gypsy on her *New York Times* bestselling memoir in 2025. (And Michele and I are together again on this book that you are currently reading.)

I also started filming and hosting my own A+E show, *Monster in My Family.* And my humble little podcast, which I used to record on the fly in my dressing room, became a scripted series starring Dennis Quaid as my father . . . with me as executive producer. *Shattered Silence* and my podcast were the source materials. Finally, in 2025, I recorded *Shattered Silence* in audiobook form. Reading my old words from so long ago was humbling and revealed the progress that came out of pain.

True crime is a big business—the books, the podcasts, the

documentaries, the movies—and it's where I've found a home. I was hardly on the inside in 1995; I was looking up news clips about my father's crimes in newspapers in the downtown library. Today I find myself firmly entrenched in the other camp. I am fully aware of my obligations as I work on all my shows, as I write about others, cast actors as real people, strive to make an entertaining production. I never forget that this is profiting off a family's pain: there are moral dilemmas there, and I do my best to err on the side of what is right and fair and good.

There is no choice when you are a secondary victim of a crime—no one ever wants their name out there associated with a killer. That is what eventually spurred me on to my entire career; I wanted to allow victims to tell the story in their own way. So I always make a heartfelt promise to honor the person's story and tell it the way they want it told.

It is an incredible privilege to be entrusted with the stories of others, a responsibility I take seriously. My father, by the way, still likes to write me letters calling me "Missy the liar." He thinks he intimidates me by keeping tabs on me from jail, sporadically contacting me to accuse me of being histrionic and attention-seeking and "making a living out of being Keith Jesperson's daughter."

I'm not making a living out of being the daughter of a serial killer. I am a woman who has built a career helping others shatter their silence, who also happens to have a father who is a serial killer. It's important to tell your story. It's even more important to know when it's time to stop telling it.

CASE #2

DIANE DOWNS, THE MONSTROUS MOTHER

THE CRIME

The small team of emergency medical providers—a doctor, a nurse, an LPN, and a night receptionist—at the McKenzie-Willamette ER in sleepy Springfield, Oregon, faced a horrifying scene on the night of May 19, 1983. Around 10:30 PM, staff heard honking and calls for help in the driveway in front of the ER. Outside, an injured young blonde woman stood next to a shiny new red Nissan Pulsar. Three children inside the car had been shot.

Frantic calls went out for help from the nearby hospital; a thoracic surgeon and a pediatric surgeon were summoned. Seven-year-old Cheryl was pronounced dead at the scene; eight-year-old Christie and three-year-old Danny were gravely injured, fighting for their lives. The woman identified herself as Diane Downs and claimed that a "shaggy-haired stranger" had shot at her car while she was out with her three children on an evening drive. A non-life-threatening bullet wound on the mother's arm was tended to.

Diane called her parents, who lived nearby; in fact, she and her kids had relocated to Oregon from Arizona only a couple of months before to be near them. Her distraught mother sat with her in the waiting room as staff raced around. When a police officer showed up, Diane claimed that the stranger had demanded her car and shot everyone inside when she refused to give it up. Diane and her father accompanied officers to a lonely road out by a river to point out where the crime had occurred. Dogs and cops and Lane County sheriff's officers soon flooded the scene; a huge investigation was launched.

Back at the hospital, Diane appeared to be sober and in control of herself. She was more than cooperative with all who spoke to her. Diane spent a sleepless night in a hospital bed; her first call that morning was to the post office in her previous hometown—Chandler, Arizona—where she asked to speak to her former lover, a married man. She broke the news of the shootings and told him she loved him; meanwhile, her ex-husband and the children's father, Steve Downs, flew to the scene.

Diane continued to talk incessantly through follow-up interviews. Her demeanor and inconsistencies in the story raised numerous red flags; physical evidence wasn't adding up. Steve suspected his ex-wife from the start. Miraculously, both Danny and Christie survived. Five weeks after the shootings, after an arduous recovery, they were released to foster homes after Diane lost them in a custody hearing. Their mother was the main suspect, and she knew it . . . but didn't seem to care. Television cameras loved the striking blonde, and a star was born. The prosecutors tried to ignore the media circus and painstakingly built their case.

Diane Downs was arrested at her parents' home in February 1984 and taken to Lane County Jail. At the time, she was six months pregnant by an unidentified father. The headlines blared in huge type nationwide: POLICE SAY DOWNS SHOT CHILDREN FOR BOYFRIEND. In opening statements at her trial in May, it became clear that the testimony of fragile daughter and eyewitness survivor Christie Downs would be crucial. With her mother sitting in front of her, she testified that Diane had shot Cheryl, then Danny. "Who shot you?" the prosecutor asked. "My mom," Christie replied through tears. As if that wasn't dramatic enough, Robert Knickerbocker, one of Diane's many married lovers, spoke for hours on the stand. Diane's own diary entries also painted a devastating picture of Knickerbocker being the man she was obsessed with and the one she hoped to be with if she didn't have children "in the way."

After a six-week trial, Diane Downs was found guilty on five charges (two counts of attempted murder, two counts of first-degree assault, and one count of murder in the first degree). The motive, the prosecutor said succinctly, was "Stress, the defection of Robert 'Nick' Knickerbocker, money problems, past history."

Diane gave birth to a daughter who she named Amy. With no disclosure of paternity, the infant was immediately taken into custody by the state and later adopted. Two months later, Diane was sentenced to life plus fifty years. Surviving children Christie and Danny Downs were adopted and raised by the man who prosecuted their mother, Fred Hugi, and his wife.

THE VICTIMS

Cheryl Downs: Age seven.

Christie and Danny Downs suffered grave injuries from the shooting; Christie still has speech difficulties and Danny remains paralyzed from the waist down.

TODAY

Diane Downs remains incarcerated at the Central California Women's Facility in Chowchilla, California. After escaping from an Oregon prison in 1987 and evading capture for ten days, she was later transferred out of state due to security concerns. She has been denied parole multiple times, most recently in 2025, and continues to maintain her innocence.

THE MEDIA

The trial of Diane Downs, her conviction, and her subsequent escape from an Oregon prison made enormous headlines all over the country. Americans could not get enough of the story of the original "monster mom."

Small Sacrifices (1987). Written by Ann Rule, the book shot to bestsellerdom. This character study of a filicidal mother who did the unthinkable cemented Rule's place as America's most popular true crime writer; she enjoyed this reputation for decades to come.

Small Sacrifices: A True Story (1989). Two years later, a 1989 made-for-TV movie based on Rule's book starred Farrah Fawcett as Diane and Ryan O'Neal as her lover who simply did not want kids. Fawcett was nominated for an Emmy as Outstanding Lead Actress for her chilling portrayal; the production won a prestigious Peabody Award for "a drama of unusual power."

My Mother's Sins (2019). Becky Babcock, Diane's youngest child who had been adopted shortly after birth, appeared on a two-hour *20/20* special featuring a reunion with author Ann Rule, who said she knew the identity of Becky's father, a long-held secret.

LEFT BEHIND

Steve Downs, ex-husband and father

Rebecca Babcock, youngest daughter, born while Diane was in prison

CHAPTER 2

WHEN MOMMY IS THE MURDERER

LEFT BEHIND: EX-HUSBAND STEVEN DOWNS

I think I love them even more than you now . . . Danny says he's my best buddy, and I'm his best buddy.
—note in Diane Downs's diary to married lover Robert Knickerbocker

As I was only three years old in 1983, I missed the media storm surrounding Diane Downs, who was convicted of killing her own daughter and grievously wounding her other two small children. The monster mother who murders her own child was a novel and truly shocking development at the time, decades before Susan Smith and Casey Anthony would make headlines around the world.

There was no true crime industry in those days; no podcasts, no internet sleuths gathering in chat rooms trading theories and sharing clues, no ID channel, no Netflix docs. Americans got their information from newspapers, television news, and books. And if there was ever a queen of the true crime book, it would be Ann Rule, a former law enforcement officer in Seattle who single-handedly boosted an entire genre. Her account of her personal relationship with serial killer Ted Bundy, *The Stranger Beside Me*, was her first book and an immediate *New York Times* bestseller. She would go on to write an astounding thirty-four more bestselling books. *Small Sacrifices* (1987) was an enormous hit, as was the TV movie based on her account.

As an adult, while my career in true crime progressed over the years, I was always fascinated by this case. Maybe because it happened in my neck of the woods: rural Oregon, while I was nearby in Spokane, Washington. Maybe because I was thankful that I had had a kind, gentle, and loving mother myself; maybe because after becoming a mother, such a crime was simply unimaginable, inured though I was to grisly murders by this point.

Two people in this case particularly interested me: innocent family members who were truly left behind and lived quite anonymously. Diane's ex-husband Steven Downs, who had not been heard from publicly for years and years was the first; Diane's biological daughter Becky was the second. I reached out to both to see if either might be interested in appearing on my podcast. I studied Ann Rule's iconic book *Small Sacrifices* like a bible when I was researching. It was the definitive account of this case; and Ann Rule was not one to shirk doing research. She had incredible access; she interviewed every possible witness or person involved in this crime, and she sat in the courtroom every day of Diane's trial. Except for Steve Downs . . . she never reached out to him.

"I don't know that woman; I had never spoken to her in my life," he said flatly in one of our first phone calls.

"Wait, you never spoke to her while she was writing the book?" I asked. I was incredulous. "You're all over that book, dialogue, your POV, you name it!" I checked again, just to be sure. Yes, countless passages starting with "Steve says . . ." complete with quotation marks. They must have come from another source, because Steve explained to me that he had only heard from her once, through intermediaries at *The Oprah Winfrey Show*, many years before.

"Producers from Oprah Winfrey called and wanted to see if I would come on the show with Ann Rule. They would do it via satellite hookup with Diane. I didn't have any interest in that whatsoever, but I had, for some time, wanted to connect with Ann Rule simply because she had written a book that definitely impacted my life, and basically became the accepted storyline. And without ever speaking to me, not one syllable, nothing. I wanted to find out about that, what she was thinking.

"One of the producers connected me with her. When I finally did speak with her, my questions were, one, how could she write a story without getting the full scope of the story, and at least another perspective—my side of it, or regarding me. Two, I did say to her, 'This is a story that impacted Christie and Danny. So what exactly are you going to share with them, since they gave so much for this storyline?' Yes, I meant monetarily. I mean, they damn near paid with their lives.

"She wanted to end the conversation right then and there; she didn't have anything to say beyond that. Not an apology, not anything. She just took her creative license and used that as carte blanche to write what she needed to write, I guess," he said. The show aired in 1988 without Steve's participation. By this point, he was long resigned to the unfairness of having his story taken away from him. No wonder he was leery of speaking to me.

In speaking with Steve, I found that in his case, *Small Sacrifices* got a few matters really wrong. Certainly, that can happen for various reasons, but I find authors and producers can often forget they are dealing with real live people. It can be a trap of perceiving it as a drama; with family members simply stock characters. I believe that Ann Rule took Diane's word on what happened, particularly in her portrayal of

Steve. And as I would come to find out for myself, Diane was far from a reliable narrator.

Steve is employed in the building trades, quietly lives in the Southwest, and has been married for many years to a lovely woman. To me, he is a warm and likable person whom I gradually got to know over our series of conversations. I was impressed that Steve took so much accountability for his own actions and part in his family; and I appreciated that. Much of his story was truly heartbreaking, and not what the public "knows."

Like me, Steve remembers the "before," early years with our families, however troubled, when we were just like everybody else: growing up, making friends, taking jobs, and finding first loves. The fateful day that changed Steve Downs's destiny came when he was a teenager on a country road in Arizona.

Steve's first glimpse of Diane was of her riding a horse called Blaze, her long blonde hair flying in the desert air as if she were the heroine on the cover of a Western-themed Harlequin paperback. At fifteen, she was a natural, navigating Blaze along Ridge Road, across from the ten-acre farm where sixteen-year-old Steve was working at the time. It was summertime, prime time for a teenage romance. On cue, Diane brought Blaze down to a slow trot. Steve smiled at her . . . and so it began.

"When I think back on it, I am in awe of what an innocent time that was, such a pure time in our lives," Steve said. "It's hard to relive and think about because of what I now know would transpire in the future. Who would've known it would've ended the way it did?"

Diane was the oldest of five children in a solid Arizona family. Her father served as the postmaster in Springfield; his word was law. Wes was a strict disciplinarian who kept a tight lid on his oldest daughter. "We were robots as kids; we were told what to do and expected to do it," Diane recalled bitterly in *Small Sacrifices*. Unsurprisingly, Diane's parents took a dim view of her dating. "Her sister seemed to be excited that Diane had a boyfriend," Steve told me, "but her mother came up with reasons for us to not be together."

Once Steve and Diane began having sex, Diane confided that her father was threatening to move the family away because Steve was becoming a "problem." Diane had many problems—she eventually told her new boyfriend that her father had sexually violated her for several years. Later she publicly recanted those claims, and both of her parents denied that any abuse occurred. After her crimes, Diane Downs underwent psychiatric evaluation, and while no single, definitive diagnosis was universally established, experts consistently described a pattern of personality traits associated with narcissistic, histrionic, and antisocial functioning—marked by attention-seeking behavior, emotional incongruity, and a striking lack of empathy. When she told Steve that her father said that he was "training her for her future husband," Steve was outraged. He swore to Diane that he'd protect her; he'd challenge her father physically if he had to and never let him hurt her again. "It seemed to me that was not exactly the kind of accusation a fifteen- or sixteen-year-old would just think up," Steve said. "And I never ever once doubted it."

Steve's reputation at the time was one more of brawn than brains. "You know the saying, 'If you're going to be dumb, you got to be strong'? Well, that was me, lifting and carrying around a three-fifty Chevy engine and walking it around sixty, seventy feet, just to show off my strength," Steve said, laughing.

The strained relationship between Steve and Wes grew more contentious as Wes flagrantly spouted his religious beliefs at the teenager, becoming ever more judgmental, opinionated, and out of line. This, while Steve noted, "I don't remember them going to church regularly." All of Steve's protective instincts, fueled by lust and teenage love, were aroused. "I might have even told her I'd marry her one day just to save her."

The strained encounters between the two men in Diane's life came to an end when Steve enlisted in the Navy while Diane attended a Baptist Bible college in California. The relationship eventually ended, only to rekindle when Steve's tour ended and both returned home. Steve was doing electrical work and other odd jobs and renting a small apartment in a Phoenix suburb, while Diane was living at her parents' home an hour away. Steve and Diane were now more mature, more sexually charged, and even more upsetting to Wes.

Diane was eighteen now, legally an adult, but Steve was soon reminded of the hold and total control Wes had over his daughter. Diane's behavior became increasingly nervous and erratic. The paradox was sex versus her family's values: Diane wanted to have premarital sex and plenty of it. She enjoyed it, especially with Steve, but her parents' convictions were like an electric fence that trapped her inside herself.

"The first time she spent the night at my house, I woke up in the morning equally panicked that her parents would notice she wasn't at home," Steve remembered, adding that the notion still dumbfounds him as they were both working adults. "I said to Diane, 'Oh, man, we have to get you home.'

"'I can't go home, I can't go home!' Diane said, spinning around the bedroom. So she didn't. She just stayed at my place." This enraged Wes; no daughter of his would live with a man outside of marriage. "One day, I'm under a car, asking Diane to hand me a wrench, I see her staring off in the distance, watching a truck drive up the road to my place," said Steve. "It's Wes, and he gets out of the car, all nonchalant with Diane's mail in one hand and a shotgun in the other. He's got that shotgun laid straight on me, and I was trying to act like I wasn't scared, but I couldn't stop thinking, *Damn, this guy is going to shoot me right here.* And he just had small talk with Diane while the gun is on me, and he doesn't say a word to me, just keeps talking to his daughter, and then he leaves." The message was clear: "Marry my daughter . . . or else."

Within two weeks, Diane and Steve were married by the local justice of the peace. According to Steve, "Her family maybe found out through an announcement in the local newspaper, but it was as close to a shotgun wedding you could get."

FATHERHOOD: ON ONE CONDITION

"My dad was a great guy, but we were poor," Steve told me, adding that he was one of nine children. "Eleven mouths to feed—oh mercy, we were poor, uneducated. I fully intended not to bring any children into this world unless I felt secure and could properly provide for them. My mother didn't cook. She was actually a terrible mother—so, I had expectations of what kind of father I wanted to be and what kind of mother I wanted my children to have."

Not having children right away was the one big-ticket item Steve recalls discussing before he and Diane got married. "I just didn't want to be in the situation I had as a child. I wanted my children to have enough money, a clean house, and feel like they always had a home because no matter how hard my father tried, I didn't feel that way growing up."

But his headstrong new wife had her own ideas. Diane was supposedly on the pill, but "I came home from work one day," said Steve, "and she just said, 'I'm pregnant.' I was happy and unhappy at the same time, because I wasn't making money and I wasn't educated, which was putting me on track for giving my kid a tough life like I had."

The GI Bill would afford Steve the education he was finally ready to receive, so he enrolled in night school to get better trained in the electrical field. "I felt like I had to focus now with a family on the way, not just on how to provide but on how to recreate the great moments I had as a child. By the time Christie was born in 1974, I wanted her life to be made of happy memories and to be proud of me as a dad. I was still young and developing myself, but she was such an amazing little girl. I wanted her to think I was an amazing dad. I took being a parent very seriously, more seriously than I think Diane did."

Inexplicably and very much behind Steve's back, Diane suddenly enlisted in the Air Force. When Christie was about six months old, Diane left to report for duty at Lackland Air Force Base in Texas, leaving a dumbfounded Steve with emotional whiplash, a new baby, and a busy work schedule.

"I only found out about what she did about a week before she had to report. I was like, 'What are you talking about? We have an infant here. Why are you leaving?' None of it made any sense, but I couldn't do anything about it, so off she went."

Suddenly a single dad, Steve began to rely on the kindness of friends, one in particular named Samantha, with whom he became romantically involved. "I always liked Samantha, and our relationship was easy, so much less dramatic than the life I had with Diane, but I felt like I had to keep my family unit together. So when Diane called in a panic from base, saying, 'I made a huge mistake,' I did her bidding." He reached a superior of hers and explained her family situation; her stint in the Air Force had lasted all of three weeks. Diane was back home.

"Within the first two years of our marriage, we had already had a baby together, she'd been enlisted and discharged from the military, I had experienced another relationship with Samantha, and then we got back together. This was a highly charged period. When Diane returned to her mundane life, with a baby at home, we had ups and downs but settled into a routine, one that revolved around her erratic behavior." And sex . . . lots of sex. Daughter Cheryl arrived less than two years after Christie's birth. Diane and Steve went to a family planning clinic to ensure there wouldn't be any more kids. "Despite all of our problems, we established that we'd be continuing our marriage, and since sex was such a big part, she suggested our sex life would be so much more fun if I had a vasectomy," Steve explained. "The first time I had the surgery, it didn't take, and I was in a lot of pain; the doctor really screwed me up. I was not running back into the office any time soon to have it done again, but Diane wouldn't let up on the perks of it, and she insisted she didn't want more children, hated birth control, complained about her weight gain, and said taking precautions with condoms was no fun.

"Whatever it was that we couldn't quite work out on an emotional level, her wanting to have sex with me made me feel like I was special, and I could fulfill her needs in some way, even if just physical, so I went in for the second vasectomy about a year after the first. What a moron, what a dumbass I was. I just kept thinking that if I did this, we could make each other really happy. I was so stupid."

Diane found the doctor in Phoenix, a few hours' drive from where they were living in Flagstaff, and booked his appointment. After the surgery, Steve stayed overnight at his sister's house and planned to return home to his family the next day.

"I got home, and Diane wasn't there," Steve said. "The apartment was cleaned out. She had drained the bank account; the kids were gone. Her family said they didn't know where she was."

Days passed without Steve knowing where his children were, so he scoured the long-distance phone bill and found that Diane had made calls to numbers in Missouri and Texas. "Frantic, I just called the numbers I didn't recognize and managed to track her down at her uncle's house in Texas. She said she left me, left our marriage. Why would she talk me into a vasectomy knowing she was ending our marriage? What if I had wanted kids in the future or met someone else later on? Why would she leave me like that?"

DANNY

Soon enough Diane and the girls returned from Texas, and somehow the marriage endured—held together by Steve's desire to keep his family unit whole and Diane's insatiable sex drive that kept Steve completely satisfied in one area, at least.

"Sex became the focal point of our marriage after Diane came back from Texas," Steve said, clearing his throat in a way that indicated he felt awkward talking about these intimate details. "We gave each other physical pleasure, so I thought after a while we were okay." They weren't. Despite their robust marital relations, unbeknownst to Steve, while he lusted after his wife, she was enjoying a sex life with many other men—some of them her coworkers at the post office where she worked.

"One day, she just says to me, 'The vasectomy didn't work,'" Steve said, a hint of anger rising in his voice at the recollection. "She just said, 'I'm pregnant,' and expected me to believe I was the father. Given our history, I didn't trust her word. So I went to get my specimen tested and was assured by the results that there was no way I could father a child. When I went home to confront her, she refused to tell me who the father was.

"I took a shower and just let the water rain down on me, but I heard banging around. When I ran out in my towel, I saw Diane running down the driveway with the girls, then taking off in the car."

Steve followed her to the babysitter's house, where Diane dropped off the girls, and then to a stranger's trailer, reduced to skulking around its perimeter. "I had the balls to walk into this strange guy's trailer, and there they were in bed together. There it was, all there right in front of me."

Unbelievable as it may seem, still fully committed to keeping his family unit whole and being there for his kids, Steve told Diane to come home. He just couldn't give up on his little girls. "Each child is so unique," he continued. "You look in those eyes and you see these babies, and I'm far from the perfect father, but I remember lying with each child and . . . you put their hands in yours and you look at these perfect tiny little hands . . . and they're holding your finger and you observe them, how they grow, their personalities, their faces, and you think about what part of you they have. Do they have my eyes, my smile, my laugh? You fall in love with your children. From that moment on always you are holding their hands."

I asked the obvious about Diane's third child, a son: "Was this the case with Danny, since he wasn't biologically yours?"

Without hesitation, Steve replied, "It was not one centimeter different. Danny was perfect. A great little guy, a pistol. I never wanted Danny to feel anything bad about his life. I had to put Diane's past behavior behind us. I didn't want Danny or either of the girls to carry out her baggage, ever. Danny wasn't here because of anything he had done. No child makes the choice to come into the world."

Perhaps in an attempt at reparations for her frequent infidelities, mostly with married men, Diane had insisted on giving her only son the name Stephen Daniel, her husband's name. Diane was married to a man who was devoted to being the father to a baby not biologically his own and willing to forfeit his dignity to keep his family together. Unfortunately, his restless wife had her sights set on someone new, and this was not just another fling. This man's sentiments were the polar opposite of Steve's. His name was Robert "Knick" Knickerbocker. Over the course of their torrid affair that began in the most mundane place, beneath fluorescent lights and beside sorting bins, he would frequently utter four words to Diane that would change the course of the lives of countless people: "I don't want children."

Diane and Knickerbocker met in Arizona around 1981 through their shared work environment connected to the United States Postal Service. Their relationship began as an affair, but from early on it was imbalanced, with Diane becoming deeply attached while Knickerbocker remained inconsistent and ultimately resistant. He made it clear he did not want children, which became a critical point of conflict.

By 1982, Knickerbocker was actively pulling away and attempting to end the relationship. Diane, however, continued pursuing him, and her behavior escalated into persistent and intrusive contact. By late 1982 into early 1983, he had fully distanced himself and recommitted to his wife, expressing concern about Diane's behavior.

Diane and Steve's increasingly tumultuous marriage led to the inevitable divorce. This did not change Steve's desire to remain a father. But Diane had her own agenda. According to him, Diane dangled the children like carrots, luring him, threatening him, punishing him. She used them to cut deals with her husband, deals that have become Steve's lifelong demons. As part of the divorce settlement, Steve bought Diane out of their house, and Diane bought a trailer of her own. Christie, Cheryl, and Danny lived with Steve full time, unofficially, as Diane retained custodial rights.

The relationship had always been unpredictable, but after the divorce, Steve described Diane's behavior as "blindsiding." With the three children living in a home with their father, Diane's sister acted as babysitter to help the children get to school. While Steve built a business, Diane delivered mail, lived in her trailer, and carried on her all-consuming affair.

Steve said that Diane harassed him for the duration of her time in Arizona: "She broke into my house, using the key her sister had, had sex in my bed with multiple men, ate my food, and threw out my bills. It was like she was saying, 'Here you go, motherfucker, have some of this.'"

Still, Steve persevered. "I used to take the kids out with me and drive around in my big white-and-red Ford four-by-two truck," he told me. "There is only so much television you can watch together, so when I had the kids, I'd try to create experiences with them that we could share, similar experiences I had when I was young, like my dad teaching me to drive.

"Danny was so cute," Steve continued, his giddiness punctuating yet another memory. "In the truck, I'd let him stand beside me with his hand on the wheel, and he'd try to push my hand away, demanding, 'I'm driving.' It was such an amazing moment, such an innocent, golden moment with him. And with Cheryl and Christie, I'd put them on the forklift at work and let Danny 'drive' it. When I remember those moments, I am right back there." But these moments were not to last.

"One day, I pull up home from work, and I find Diane, her mother and father, and my kids all packed up," Steve said, his voice cracking with bitterness. Diane told Steve she was moving the children with her to Oregon.

"What? Why?" Steve cried, before pulling Diane out of earshot of the children. "I never liked to fight in front of the kids, and this was one conversation I didn't want them to hear."

"Why are you doing this? What the hell is going on?" Steve asked. He said he begged Diane to leave the kids with him, as they were still in school and would adjust more easily if Diane went ahead of them to get settled in her new life in Oregon. "Let me come and be with you all for the summer," Steve had tried to rationalize with Diane.

"I think the main reason Diane didn't leave them with me was to save face with her parents. I suspect she was thinking, *What kind of mother leaves her children in Arizona?* and her parents would judge her for that. I knew her taking them with her was not because she wanted them there. It was all about impression management," Steve told me.

In May 1983, Diane moved to Oregon, where Knickerbocker was already living with his wife in the Springfield area. This relocation appears directly tied to her continued fixation on him rather than a neutral job transfer. In the approximately six weeks following her move, she attempted to reestablish contact while he maintained his rejection.

What Steve didn't know was that along with the children's clothes and other belongings, Diane had packed up Steve's .22 rifle, a .38 pistol, a .22 pistol, and a shotgun. The move took place, very much against Steve's wishes. Their new family life in another state, where Diane had transferred jobs and would work as a mail carrier, would last only six weeks.

Two weeks before the shooting, Steve had tickets to fly up to Oregon to see his children. "I had some real trouble happening at work and a bunch of fires to put out, so I canceled the trip," Steve said, and then added sadly, "I didn't know my time would be so limited."

THE CALL

"Diane and the kids have been shot. Hope you're happy." This was the anonymous call Steve received on May 19, 1983, after Diane drove her three blood-drenched children to the ER in Springfield.

When Steve arrived in Portland, he was hit with newspaper headlines displayed everywhere before he even exited the airport. He read for the first time about the "shaggy-haired stranger," but far more shocking, the fact that one of his children had been killed during what Diane said was a carjacking. "I just had a weakness come over me, and then melting," said Steve, before he took several moments to collect himself.

The details of the incident continued to blindside Steve, especially the detectives finding casings of a .22 caliber weapon. "I called my roommate and asked him to go to where I had my guns hidden to see if the .22 was there. None of my guns were there. I hadn't noticed because I hadn't gone hunting in a while, but she took them when she took the kids from my house to Oregon."

With Diane and her children the victims of a crazed killer, the Downs family rallied around the bereaved mother, who sat in a hospital bed with a sling around her arm as Christie and Danny clung to life. "Here I am with no support up against Wes and the rest of the Fredricksons, just wanting to see my daughter Cheryl, but they were conducting an autopsy and then Diane had her cremated without my knowledge. I never saw her," Steve said. "I just saw her casket at the funeral."

The hospital, as Steve recalled, was a whirlwind of close calls, beeping machines, alarms sounding off, resuscitations, and diagnoses of Danny's paralysis and Christie's life-altering stroke. "You watch them scrape the bottom of your three-year-old's foot with a metal tool and see nothing, no movement, and then from the other room, you hear them trying to bring your eight-year-old back to life, all while the Downs family is defending Diane," Steve told me.

"I love Danny. I always have," Steve reiterated. His feelings got the best of him, and he called out Danny's biological father, a man whose identity he was well aware of. "He was one of these mama's boys, and he was young. I mean, he was probably five years younger than I was, somewhere around there. He probably knew from watching the news what had happened. But when I called, he didn't really respond like I would expect him to. I said, 'Right now Danny needs us. He needs all of us. He needs everybody in his life because he's paralyzed. He's hurting.'

"'I don't want to have anything to do with it,' were his words. I reminded him, 'This is your son. This is your biological son.' I don't know what kept me from kicking the hell out of him, because he needed it right then. He needed it before, but right then, he needed it even worse. Because he really showed the real color of who he was, a real weak piece of shit." True to his word, this young man stayed far, far away from the situation as Steve tried to cope.

It wasn't long before the police determined Diane was lying about the "shaggy-haired stranger." After the Lane County Sheriff's Office, led by Detective Doug Welch, cleared Steve of the crime, confirming his unshakable alibi, they began to find further inconsistencies in Diane's story. The more she spoke, the less her story added up. Once they read her diary, Detective Welch sniffed out the motive: Diane wanted her married lover Knickerbocker to start a new life with her, but Christie, Cheryl, and Danny were in the way. If Knickerbocker wasn't going to be a father to anyone's children, she had to get rid of them.

"The price that people pay, little children, innocent children pay for the sickness that surrounds them," said Steve sorrowfully.

While Diane was on bail awaiting the pretrial, Steve began prepping the life he would take his children back to in Arizona. He made frequent visits to Oregon to see his children, who were temporarily placed in foster care with the Slaven family. Steve vividly remembered being surveilled by Diane and her brother, Paul, who to this day remains a staunch defender of his sister's innocence. They talked him into allowing Diane to see the children, which would violate a court order issued by Judge

Gregory Foote. If he did this one thing, Diane said, she wouldn't stand in Steve's way when he sought full custody of Christie and Danny—as if she had any say in the matter. "I made a deal with the devil," recalled Steve. "Christie wanted to see her mother, and I thought, *Well, Paul will be there,* so I agreed."

They arranged to meet at Diane's parents' house, where Diane was staying. "About three or four hours later, I see Diane and Christie getting into a car, and that wasn't part of the deal. I was thinking maybe she was trying to get rid of the witness," said Steve. (Christie was an eyewitness for the prosecution.) "I understand why anyone would think I was the bad guy back then, because I was; I made a deal with the goddamn devil, and she had no intention of [ever] releasing those kids to me."

Christie and Danny would later go to live with and be officially adopted by the Hugi family. Quite unusual, given that Fred Hugi was the state's prosecutor in Diane's case. To many it seemed like a conflict of interest. In any event, it was upheld. The court had ruled that the aftermath of the crime and the health needs of Christie and Danny were too much for Steve to handle—something that should have been decided with Steve's input, but he did not put up a custody fight.

At this point, it was Steve's understanding that if he didn't sign away his parental rights, Christie and Danny would remain in the foster care system with a likelihood of being separated. Adoption was a more viable option for the siblings to remain together.

"The more the case worker painted a picture of my children's future, the more it felt like pressure. I was asked, 'Do you love your kids? Do you love your kids enough to do the right thing, what's right for them, what's going to be right for them now? Or are you just trying to hold on and get in the way and make their lives even more miserable by putting them in a more dire situation by holding on to what you cannot have?'"

By way of background, after the shooting, still under Diane's sway, Steve made the mistake of allowing her unsupervised contact with the children, which resulted in his loss of custody. So, what Steve heard was, "You're not getting those kids back to Arizona."

"They had deemed me a shitty parent," Steve told me. "The only thing that Christie and Danny had was each other. And they were going to be taken away from each other if I didn't sign away parental rights. That was my thinking at the time. I love them with all my heart. The thing of it is, people don't know who I am or what I'm capable of and how much I love those children. I would've spent the rest of my life taking care of them. I feel so responsible because I should've . . . I should've . . . I should've done something more to stop her from taking those kids to Oregon."

Diane Downs has been denied parole four times. Each board cited her as being dangerous and a public risk. Members of the parole boards took note of Diane's lack of accountability and empathy for her crimes and denial of guilt. I remembered Steve telling me he would have been more than willing to testify against her. By doing so, he would finally have a voice and share with the parole board and Diane, herself, his true feelings and how her actions have impacted his life. He called it a life sentence, adding:

"She stole Cheryl's life. She destroyed Christie's and Danny's in the process. And here she is wanting to get out of prison. I know I live in a prison every day. I'm not getting out of it any time soon. Christie isn't; Danny isn't. We're going to live our lives out in this prison, and maybe it's a different prison than Diane's particular surroundings, but make no mistake, it's a prison," he said.

"There was a time when I wanted to protect Diane," Steve told me in one of our last conversations, his voice cutting in and out through the Bluetooth speaker of his car. Forty years later, the "should'ves, would'ves, could'ves" still rattle him from his sleep. If he had pulled the fire alarm, he thinks things would be different now. So many of Steve's sentiments are laced with the poison of self-blame. Did he betray his parental duty just as Diane had? That is an unbearable type of burning regret that cannot be extinguished. "I made so many goddamn mistakes," he told me, his words trailing off.

CHAPTER 3

WHEN A KILLER GIVES LIFE

LEFT BEHIND: DAUGHTER BECKY BABCOCK

The more a daughter knows about the details of her
mother's life, the stronger the daughter.
—Anita Diamant, *The Red Tent*

The world of secondary victims is an insular, close-knit one; for many years, I had been aware of Rebecca "Becky" Babcock, and our paths crossed several times as she navigated the media machine. Becky, of course, had been in the harshest imaginable spotlight in utero: while a heavily pregnant Diane Downs was on trial and sentenced. The whole world was abuzz with rumors about the identity of her child's father.

A fertile woman who had once served as a surrogate mother for a childless couple, Diane was quite savvy about her reproductive cycle. Having gotten pregnant while awaiting her trial, most onlookers deemed this pregnancy a cynical and calculated move to engender sympathy for a supposedly grieving mother. The infant was named Amy Elizabeth, sharing in Diane's legal first name, Elizabeth Diane, and she was taken away from Diane immediately after her birth, adopted into a loving family, and renamed Rebecca.

Becky lived in relative anonymity for many years, but as I delved deeply into the case, once again using *Small Sacrifices* as my casebook and speaking with many of the players, I became increasingly intrigued by her story. I, of all people, understood what it felt like to be the daughter of a killer, to agonize about the DNA we shared with a monstrous parent. And I couldn't help but have Steve Downs's words ring in my ear: "No child makes the choice to come into the world."

Becky's reintroduction to the general public started with an article in *Glamour* magazine, "I Found Out My Mother Was a Killer: The Rebecca Babcock Story."

Journalist Eric Mason teamed up with reporter Lisa Grace Lednicer from the *Oregonian*, the local paper that had followed the Downs story from day one. The two wrestled with how best to present Becky's story, not wanting to do another tawdry, sensational piece about a notorious killer. This, they decided, would be more of a family story, about secrets and how they affect everyone, especially an innocent daughter born into infamy. Both were cognizant of their great responsibility to the woman who was about to share the biggest secret in her life, much against her family's wishes. The article, which reads as a long-form personal essay, was published in May 2010 to great fanfare. The 1984 *Washington Post* article "The Mother and the Mystery" stood in stark contrast to the *Glamour* feature. Decades earlier, the question was why Diane did it. By 2010, the question had changed: what did it do to the people who survived her?. Becky's identity was officially out there in the world.

Just as they had with Steve Downs more than two decades before, an *Oprah* producer came knocking. Becky agreed to make an appearance on the show later that year; the focus was very much on her mother's case. Her physical resemblance to Diane, particularly the large, expressive eyes, was undeniable. After that show aired, Becky worked as a health aide and lived a relatively quiet life for nearly a decade. In 2019, she participated in a *20/20* special called "My Mother's Sins." The premise for the show was heavily hyped . . . Becky wanted to know who her biological father was. Only Ann Rule knew, but she had passed away in 2015, the identity of Becky's father buried with her.

In 2010, ABC arranged a meeting between Rebecca Babcock and Ann Rule—the author who had written her mother's story—bringing them face-to-face for the first time on *20/20*. Ann was supposedly to reveal this big secret.

"Do you know who my father is?" Becky asked, her voice searching to be unburdened from what she had been carrying for a lifetime.

"Yes, I do," Rule answered.

"Can you tell me?"

"No, I can't."

Then, in a moment that viewers could sense hurt more than it helped, the author told her, "I've met your father. He's a lovely, nice guy." But that was as far as she would go. In *Small Sacrifices* Rule had written that Becky's biological father was a man on Diane Downs's postal route, one random hookup. Getting pregnant was easy: Diane reportedly seduced the man with some whiskey and cigars. The bestseller would remain the only documentation of Becky's origin story.

I watched the show with mixed emotions. I could only think: *What a cruel move, why lure Becky onto a TV show with such a promise, then refuse to let her know the answer?* The disappointing lack of candor on Ann Rule's part made me want to get involved. "I know, but I won't tell you . . ." was a pointless exercise.

When Becky and I spoke we had a long conversation about her reality: that as her biological mother is the infamous Diane Downs, half her genes come from a woman who is essentially evil—and mentally troubled as well. She still had no idea who her father was, which tormented her. The other half of her genetic parentage remained a mystery.

I asked what I thought was a logical question when Becky kept saying to me, "I wonder who my dad is." I said, "Let's ask your mom." Becky had been in sporadic touch with Diane over the years and warned me that she could be quite erratic and paranoid. But nothing ventured, nothing gained. I sent a letter off to Diane in prison.

When I opened the card I received in October 2019, four Q-tips wrapped in plastic fell out. The enclosed note said:

> Melissa, I received your letter. I've no desire to plead my case on a podcast. Usually I'm done with the conversation at this point but since I received a letter from Rebecca Babcock saying she's working with you on this I need to caution you against endorsing lies that will follow your career long after the truth is known. Already I know you won't hear anything I have to say, so I'm sending you something to look at. Please find my cheek swabs enclosed. Lane County has my DNA. California entered my DNA into the national DNA crime database, Scotland Yard and the FBI have my DNA. Will it hurt if you have it too?
>
> I was adopted in the 1950s. If you run my DNA through DEN database you'll find a match with my half sister in Oregon. She, her son, and her daughter were disinherited by her father in 2017 just before he died. I was not. If you share my paternity with Rebecca Babcock the only reason she'd refuse a DNA test is because she knows she's not my daughter. For all I know, she's my disinherited niece trying to con me out of Amy's inheritance. Maybe you can learn the truth she hides.

I didn't even know where to start with all this. Diane had been behind bars for more than three decades at this point, and it seemed that her mental capacity had declined over the years. Always noted for her sharp intelligence and volubility, it was clear to me that she was no longer entirely coherent. I had done extensive research on the entire case, and I certainly didn't believe Diane was adopted. She looked so much like her father, for one thing. And Diane's brother James, an avid supporter and defender of his sister to this day, had certainly never mentioned such a possibility. That was the end of our communications.

I tossed the letter into an old black metal three-drawer filing cabinet in my basement, which felt like the appropriate place for correspondence like this. It's where I had kept my father's letters, some opened, others untouched, until last winter when I fed them to the fire in my backyard. The flames consumed them the way a forest fire scours a landscape—violent, but purifying—so that something new might grow in the space they left behind.

Becky had been adopted shortly after her birth by a couple with a four-year-old daughter. Given the name Rebecca, she lived in an idyllic home on eighty acres near a river. Becky and her older sister enjoyed horses, riding, 4-H, and animals, which were ubiquitous as they grew up. By all accounts, including Becky's, her parents were caring and loving. Though Becky always knew she and her sister were adopted, the identity of her biological mother was kept a secret. This was not a revelation her parents wanted to share. From the time she was eight years old, Becky pestered her adopted mother, who would only say her birth mother was a troubled woman who had done bad things. Her mom continued to put her off, believing she was not mature enough to handle this knowledge. But clues were dropped, and hints were overheard over the years.

On July 11, 1987, Diane Downs escaped prison by scaling the twelve- to fifteen-foot chain-link fence surrounding the women's facility while guards weren't looking. She used clothing to cover the barbed wire at the top and dropped down the other side. She remained at large for ten days as authorities launched a multi-state manhunt. Becky's parents feared Diane would try to find Becky and kidnap her. After Diane's recapture, as a precaution, Becky's parents informed their babysitter about who Becky's birth mother was and to be on high alert because if Diane escaped once, they feared she could do it again.

When Becky was eleven, she tricked her longtime babysitter into revealing the name of her birth mother. Once she had the name, it was off to the bookstore. "I had to have my parents take me, obviously, because I just was a kid. I found the book by Ann Rule, and I thumbed through the pages and went straight to the pictures. That was like the moment reality set in that this woman is actually my biological mom. [By this time] it had been three years of asking. I didn't think I'd ever know, and at that point I wished I hadn't. It was really scary. I just kind of buried it deep." And there the secret stayed, until Becky got her first boyfriend at the age of sixteen.

"He asked if there was anything that I never told anybody before, you know, a secret. I told him who Diane Downs was—that was the biggest secret I had. One day he said, 'You know, let's watch a movie. Come on over to my house.' I remember sitting on his futon and he popped the tape in and then left the room to go make snacks or something. That's when it started playing . . . *Small Sacrifices*. It was difficult to watch Farrah Fawcett as Diane Downs, and to let that story unfold in front of me. I did not want to watch, but I couldn't stop.

"The part that really got me was when Diane was holding that baby . . . a representation of *me*. It became real. I don't even know the words to explain how it felt. It killed a little part of my innocence in a sense. I felt so stupid looking back, wanting to know for so long. I understood why my mom didn't want to tell me. It affected me greatly, because that was the beginning of my rebellious years. Perhaps that information and not dealing with it appropriately and emotionally it caused me to go off the rails a little bit."

And go off the rails Becky did. Always a strong-minded child, her rebellious ways took a dark turn. "Partying, sleeping around, drugs, running away . . ." she told me. "I was no longer living at home at that point. It was scary. Looking back now, I'm amazed I'm still alive after some of the situations I put myself in. After I saw the video and really got the full idea of who Diane Downs was, I just kind of stopped caring. I shut down inside somehow."

By the time she was seventeen years old, Becky knew she was going nowhere and felt she was a complete disappointment to her family. She was determined to turn her life around. In an odd echo of Diane's history, she impulsively joined the Army and shipped off to boot camp. During the battery of tests all recruits underwent, it was determined she was pregnant. A superior called her father to break the news. There would be no military service; motherhood was upon her.

Becky's parents were as supportive as they could be. "They said, you know, we raised our children. This is something you need to do on your own." However, they did pay rent on a house for two years so she could raise her baby—her dad insisted that every parent needs to be home for at least the first two years. Their financial assistance made it possible for Becky to be a hands-on mom. And she loved it.

"At the beginning, as a new mom, I didn't have time to think—sleep deprived and always caring for a little baby. I never really worried about my genes transferring to him. He was perfect in my eyes. Maybe it's how my mom felt when she looked at me, you know, and accepted me as is. I just saw this perfect little baby; I didn't worry who he was going to grow up to be."

A couple of years later, in a steady relationship with a coworker, Becky got pregnant by choice a second time. Adjusting to pregnancy was hard on the relationship; it quickly fell apart. Then one day, the father of her child simply left with little or no warning. "I was just destroyed. I was heartbroken. I was pregnant with my second child. It was a high-risk pregnancy; I was bedridden for most of it. I couldn't afford where I was living because I couldn't work. I ended up staying in a homeless shelter."

Becky sought her parents' input. After a family discussion, she decided the best option would be to put this baby up for adoption. She was living in a shelter and had no way to provide for two children. "I didn't want to give my son away, but it was what was best for both of them," she said sadly. Becky moved in with her parents until the baby was born.

The birth of Becky's second child was emotionally and physically challenging. "He was perfect. They told me that I could spend as much time with him as I wanted . . . I knew that if I didn't let go immediately, that I would never let him go. I was devastated, and I didn't know who to talk to. I didn't know anybody else who had put their child up for adoption and had that loss.

"One night, I was especially sad, and I wondered if Diane ever felt what I felt in that moment. I just needed somebody that I could relate to. I didn't need a mother; I had one, but I needed somebody that had been through it, and she went through it with me. There was that connection. She was my biological mom who held me and who let me go. For that brief moment, I just wanted to know that she was human."

It was at this low point that Becky reached out to Diane. "After I put that letter in the mailbox, my heart sank. What did I do? Why? Why did I do that? I was terrified of what the letter coming back would say, but it was an excited terrified." Diane responded in a fairly normal fashion, describing her physical appearance, talking about where she'd been born, her tone pleasant. "I got the letter and I was like, Okay, this isn't so bad. Maybe I didn't make a mistake in writing her.

"I responded a few days after receiving her letter, and I think it was in this second letter that I asked about my biological father. I asked who he was and if I could know about him and where he was. Diane couldn't stand the idea that the focus was no longer on her. She just got angry and said she was never going to tell me and why would I ask those questions? I didn't need to know . . ." Her correspondence with Diane didn't last long, maybe five or six letters back and forth in total.

It was here that I entered the picture. I had an idea for Becky: that she be the featured guest on the second season of my podcast. *Happy Face*

Presents: Two Face would be the title, and it would chronicle the journey I took Becky on to find her biological father. The fantasy in her head, of course, was that there was a loving, stable family out there somewhere that her biological dad would welcome her into. This is an understandable dream when you know all too well who your biological mother is. Surely there was a decent, upstanding father out there somewhere . . . maybe even missing her?

The rest of Becky's overtures to her biological family members had not met with any success. There was the brief correspondence with Diane herself, which ended when she became angry and abusive in her letters. We talked about her half-siblings, Christie and Danny, whom she had previously contacted. "I did reach out to them back in 2006. I found Christie online. We had a little bit of a conversation going. We spoke every couple of days. She told me a little bit about herself; I told her about myself—and then one day I got a message that she and Danny didn't want anything to do with me. So much time had passed that they don't want to get to know me."

Christie and Danny were aware of Becky, knew that they were related and shared an undeniable link. Still, according to Becky, they were not interested in connecting, and the rejection stung, though Becky took it philosophically. "It's understandable—what they went through I could never even imagine, and maybe being in my life or meeting me would bring up some of that for them. I'm not sure."

Undeterred, Becky had also reached out to Diane's father, Wes, and they spoke several times. "He was a sweet man. He wanted to tell me a lot of the family history, but he also wanted to talk about Diane and about her case and how she's innocent. I told both Diane and her father—when we first spoke years ago—that I didn't want to hear about her guilt or her innocence. I just want to hear about her, about the family. And I just want to know about my biological father!" That information was not forthcoming, from Wes or Diane.

So I asked Becky: "Knowing who your biological father is, what would that do for you?" She replied, "I almost don't want to know, because I have this side of me that is from a monster, and this other side of me that I don't know. At this point, I can think that it's good to fill in the blanks. I can decide who he is, and I can think that he's an amazing person, even if he's not. As long as he's a decent human being, I'd be happy. But I'm scared . . . What if he doesn't want me in his life?"

There were certainly no guarantees, but she was willing to find out. She had some compelling reasons to look, some of them medical. Some serious health problems had arisen, and knowing her paternal health history could help. More importantly, maybe he would want a relationship? In any case, I wanted to give her a sense of her own agency. She'd tricked her way as a kid into finding out her mother's hidden identity; she kept running into brick walls when it came to her father. I knew I could solve that mystery.

It was quite a journey; the hunt for her father and the necessary research took up almost a full year of my working life. Becky kept telling me that this could go one of two ways: good or bad. I was optimistic; I hoped for the best. I wanted that happily-ever-after ending to at least one side of this story for her. Ann Rule had passed away in 2015 so there was no returning to that source when it came to her father. We did, however, have technology and science on our side now. But first, I reached out to one more family member.

The personal meeting I arranged between Becky and Diane's brother James was fraught with tension. He had made it clear he had his own agenda; Becky, of course, had her own as well. Very shortly after our greetings and chitchat about travel, he dove right into a question Becky had struggled with years before.

James read aloud a letter he had recently received from Diane:

> I was four and a half months pregnant when I was arrested. Amy and I were locked in a jail cell alone for nearly four months before she was born. She gave me the strength to keep calm during the trial. Every day I tell her that she was going to be okay. I pat her bottom and rub her back. I didn't let myself get consumed with worry for her sake. Then, when we returned to our jail cell after my first day on the witness stand, there was a court order waiting in our concrete slab bed, the state, it seems, took custody of Amy even before she was born. The trial wasn't even over yet, and the state was taking her. I was physically ill, but couldn't dwell on it because I didn't want Amy to feel my pain. It was a different story after she was gone. I cried and cried. It felt like I lost a friend as much as a child. That's a loss from which I'll never recover.

"That's what my sister said about you," he told Becky. "I asked her to share something with me because, I told her, the world needs to understand what she felt like when she was having the baby." This was certainly the information Becky had sought when giving her own son up for adoption years before, and it belied the angry, confrontational tone of Becky's own correspondence with Diane. This was valuable information; the mood in the room softened.

But James had no interest in discussing Becky's father: "She doesn't know who the father is, and unfortunately there's only two people that do. The author [Ann Rule] didn't know who the father was because she wasn't there during conception and has never been told by my sister. The only people that know are the mother and the father of Becky. It was just some guy in her route, you know, I mean, I don't have any idea who it is. He knows or maybe he doesn't, I would imagine. So I don't know . . ." was all he was willing to say on that topic. And we soon got to his real reason for showing up.

"I could not, in any way, shape, or form, be a part of somebody's life that thought my sister was guilty. And really my life is now consumed with my sister, which is why I'm sitting here, and what I want. What I believe is that if you looked at not actions and evidence, that there would be no doubt that she would believe that she's innocent. My sister's in prison and she doesn't belong there, and I want you to be her mouthpiece. I want you to go out there and tell the world she didn't do this." There it was.

There was some anguished discussion; Becky tried in vain to tell him that she was only seeking a connection to her biological family and had no interest in relitigating Diane's case. But James was laser focused on his mission. There was not going to be a meeting of the minds here. However, James did agree to a DNA test to help Becky in her quest. For one thing, Becky wanted to settle the matter, and more DNA could only help in her quest for her father's identity. She and James even joked a little as he was departing, with him teasing her about how the Downs family was descended from Danish royalty. The DNA results left no doubt: Diane was Becky's mother. It was time to bring in a real expert.

We enlisted a detective to help, but first we spoke to Dr. Greg Hampikian, a DNA expert, to learn a bit about the process and what to expect. We found out that it was highly likely that Becky would be able to find a lot of information, because American genealogical databases are populated disproportionately with Caucasians, whereas criminal databases are not. According to Dr. Hampikian men often have a much easier time tracing lineage because women often take on their husband's last name and give their children his name as well. Men usually give their last name.

Dr. Hampikian continued to explain some of the technical aspects of examining DNA, as well as the process itself and some of the science behind it, but ultimately he suggested that we contact a genealogist—someone whose job it is to do a deep dive into the results provided by a commercial

DNA service—and really trace backgrounds and family lines by using the results as a foundation and researching beyond them.

Enter Michelle Leonard, a professional genealogist, author, and historian. "My main specialty is working with DNA testing in order to identify unknown ancestors," she told us. Just the person we needed. Michelle's belief is that documents can sometimes contain false information, but DNA evidence is more or less irrefutable. "I always follow the DNA. Always put the DNA first, and I don't let that other evidence—the documentary evidence or the hearsay evidence—cloud my judgment and lead to confirmation bias, because that information can always be wrong or falsely given. The DNA, however, will lead to the truth. At the same time, it has to be worked with correctly in order to get to the correct answer.

"DNA," she concluded, "is a very scientific way of going about a very emotional process." The process was indeed emotional; the necessary swabs were taken, and we waited with bated breath. Finally, it was time to get her report. She had swiftly identified Becky's biological father. Her news: he was a little younger than Diane, and he was still alive. Her father was just under six feet tall with dark black hair. His name was found on a US index listing an address just outside the Eugene–Springfield area in Oregon.

Becky was completely overwhelmed. "He's alive, which means that he's most likely known about me, and that's what's pretty hard for me right now. The emotional part that's just flooding right now," she said through her surprise. Michelle confirmed through old address records that this man had been living in the right place at the right time to be our target. She further explained that he was married and had a grown daughter, so Becky had another half sister, which was quite a lot to take in. Finally, Michelle confirmed that he was nothing like Diane.

"I have not been able to find anything for your biological father other than he's a successful man. He runs a business. There are no criminal records; a thirty-dollar speeding fine is the worst thing I can find for him. He is educated; he comes across as intelligent. His daughter is a high-flying person in her chosen profession. I can't find anything about the family that gives me any concerns as to who they are."

After Michelle revealed Becky's father's identity to her, including information about his immediate family, location, and other details including biological and publicly available information about him, Becky did in fact reach out to him. Carefully, through a letter, she explained very generally what her purpose was in locating him, and she gave him her number. He contacted her through what appeared to be a burner phone, and after confirming her identity and purpose, he declined to speak at length with her or answer any of her questions . . . leaving her with a vague promise that he would reach out to her after the podcast aired.

"He's known who I am for at least ten years. I've been in the media, and he's chosen to stay out of my life and continues to choose that. So I respect it. That's all I can do. He made it extremely clear that he is not interested. I mean, he used a burner phone to contact me. And the only reason I think that he even contacted me was because he knows I was looking for him, and I'm assuming he knows that I wouldn't stop until I found him. More so, I think that he contacted me to guarantee that I would not put his information out there, and as soon as I promised him I wouldn't, he didn't want anything to do with me.

"My biological father, I think, is scared, and it's understandable. I mean, he slept with an infamous killer, and it produced a child that's now gone to the media and been pretty out there. So if I were him, I guess I'd be embarrassed. It would be a secret that I would want to keep. And I think that that's what it is for him, as a secret he wants to keep, which means that I have to remain at a distance. I think that what I did get from him was probably all that I'm going to get, and it was just a bunch of promises to answer questions in the future and then telling me to never contact him again."

So . . . in the end, did I succeed or fail in trying to help Becky? I did what we had set out to do: find her father. And they did speak. In their one brief conversation, he made his feelings clear. He would keep the door open and have an in-depth conversation with her at a later time if she did not publicly out him on our podcast. That was the carrot. The unspoken alternative was lawyers. That was the stick. This man prized his good name and reputation above all else; he was embarrassed to be a part of this story at all. This man stood far from the loving father Becky dreamed would welcome her into his life. The fantasy died. Though we know who he is, neither Becky nor I would ever out him. We didn't want to be sued, of course . . . but I also saw a picture of his acknowledged daughter, who appeared to be a lovely woman with a successful career. Who was I to upend her life and spoil her image of her father, whom she no doubt loved? She is yet another innocent bystander.

But in a big way, our mission failed. Not one person involved in our quest cared about Becky herself—her understandable desire to know her parentage. Every exchange felt transactional; there were so many "ifs" in these interactions. I'll love you and be your uncle *if* . . . from her uncle James. I'll tell you all you want to know about how you came to be *if* . . . from her biological father. In the end, Becky was left with her real family, the parents who raised her and her own son.

"I set out to find him, and I did. It was disappointing, but it just reconfirms how amazing my parents are and how grateful I am that I have such loving parents. My dad would do anything to see me happy and see me smile. I know that I'm loved, and that's important. My adopted father is my real father, because he is the one who has been there for every scrape, every broken heart, every challenge in my life, and to celebrate all of the good as well. He has always been there, and he is a very, very good man. Same as my mom. She was always there for me and she still is.

"If I take nothing else from this journey, it has confirmed that they are all that I need. I don't need Diane Downs in my life. I don't need this new biological father in my life. I need my real parents, my adoptive parents: the ones that love me, the ones who chose me and would do anything to see me safe and happy."

CASE #3

JOHN EDWARD ROBINSON, THE INTERNET'S FIRST SERIAL KILLER

THE CRIME

By all outward appearances, businessman John Robinson was a solid Midwestern citizen. Married for more than three decades, he and his wife raised four children. Well liked in the community for his jovial, back-slapping ways, he was a Scoutmaster and coached a baseball team. A regular churchgoer, he taught Sunday school. He appeared to be a successful executive; he had plenty of money and various consulting businesses. He promoted philanthropy and was on the board of directors for a local charity. The local community was stunned when he was arrested in Kansas in June 2000, and the bodies of two women were found in barrels on his remote rural property. Robinson would turn out to be a most sadistic and prolific serial killer. But there were many signs along the way.

The all-American kid who had once been an Eagle Scout showed disturbing tendencies early on. While in his twenties and working as an x-ray technician for a doctor, he was arrested for stealing $33,000 from the practice and put on probation.

Court records and contemporaneous reporting, including coverage from *The Kansas City Star* and the Associated Press, as well as Ann Rule's *Anyone You Want Me to Be,* document that Robinson was charged and convicted in the 1970s and early 1980s for crimes including embezzlement, theft by deception, and check-related fraud, and repeatedly violated probation while receiving minimal jail time. In 1984, he would commit his first murder, of a young woman named Paula Godfrey, whom he had offered to help gain business skills. She vanished after being in contact with him, her parents filed a missing persons report, police interviewed him, and Robinson denied everything and continued on his path.

Women in his orbit continued to disappear until Robinson was arrested in 1987 for parole violations and fraud in both Kansas and Missouri. He remained incarcerated for several years, during which he continued to cultivate relationships and manipulate those around him. After his release in 1993, Beverly Bonner moved to Kansas to work for him. She was never heard from again. In the years that followed, Robinson—a skilled forger—continued to cash her alimony checks. By then, he had begun refining a pattern that combined exploitation, disappearance, and financial gain, often targeting vulnerable women. Robinson embraced the internet once he was free, delving deep into the disturbing world of BDSM sites and chat rooms on his five computers. He sought out submissive women who were open to master/slave arrangements. In 1999 he offered a "slave contract" to a young immigrant living in Indiana; she vanished after signing the contract and ceding control of her bank accounts to Robinson. When asked, he claimed she had been deported.

Robinson grew more and more reckless as the years passed; he became a person of interest in numerous missing persons investigations. Two charges brought about his downfall: one woman accused him of sexual assault; another of stealing her sex toys. This minor theft charge allowed investigators to obtain a search warrant for his remote Lynn County, Kansas, farm; nothing turned up until a police dog sniffed around a barrel. The two bodies stuffed inside separate barrels were discovered; across the state line in Robinson's Missouri storage unit three more chemical drums were found, with female bodies inside. All five victims had been bludgeoned to death with a blunt instrument, likely a hammer, in the head, his preferred method of killing.

In 2002, after the longest criminal trial in Kansas history, Robinson was convicted and received the death penalty for two murders and life imprisonment for another, plus various lesser charges. After his Kansas convictions, Robinson faced murder charges in Missouri based on the evidence discovered in that state. Missouri aggressively pursued capital punishment convictions, so Robinson's attorneys wanted to avoid a trial there. When it became clear that the women's remains would never be found without Robinson's cooperation—cooperation he refused to consider—a compromise was reached.

In October 2003, Robinson delivered a carefully worded plea, acknowledging that prosecutors had enough evidence to convict him of five counts of first-degree murder in Missouri. The court accepted it as a guilty plea, but observers noted what it lacked: remorse, detail, or any meaningful acceptance of responsibility. Robinson received five life sentences in Missouri for murders tied to that jurisdiction—some of which were prosecuted without recovered bodies—while separate convictions for additional victims in Kansas resulted in death sentences.

THE VICTIMS

The con man and serial killer known as "The Slavemaster" in online BDSM circles had eight known victims:

Paula Godfrey (1984): Robinson hired the nineteen-year-old woman for one of his "companies" as a sales rep; her parents' pleas to authorities after her disappearance led nowhere. In 2003, Robinson agreed to a plea that stopped short of a full confession but conceded the evidence against him in Paula Godfrey's murder. Her body has never been found.

Lisa Stasi (1985): Going by the alias John Osborne, Robinson met nineteen-year-old Lisa Stasi and her four-month-old daughter Tiffany at Hope House, a shelter for homeless women in Kansas City, where he offered to enroll the young woman into an educational program with free room and board. Lisa and baby Tiffany checked into Room 131 at the Rodeway Inn in Overland Park in early January 1985. Lisa told her relatives that "Mr. Osborne" arranged and paid for their new accommodations. Lisa Stasi was never heard from again, leading her family to believe both Lisa and Tiffany would never return home. Robinson gave Tiffany to his brother and sister-in-law. To this day, Robinson will not reveal the whereabouts of Lisa's remains.

Catherine Frances Clampitt (1987): In January 1987, Clampitt was a twenty-seven-year-old who left her child with her parents in Wichita Falls, Texas, and moved to Kansas City to live with her brother's family and find employment. Shortly after her arrival, Clampitt answered a job ad for a position at Equi II, a management consulting firm in Overland Park, Kansas, where John Robinson promised her extensive travel opportunities and a new wardrobe before hiring her. The two were seen staying at several local hotels near the Equi II offices. On June 15, 1987, Clampitt was headed to a meeting with Robinson. She has not been seen since; her missing persons case remains open.

Beverly Bonner (1994): Prison librarian Bonner met Robinson when he was an inmate in Western Missouri Correctional Center in Cameron in the late eighties. She left her husband, the prison doctor, and moved to Kansas to work for Robinson after his release. After Robinson arranged for Bonner's alimony checks to be forwarded to a Kansas post office box, Bonner's family never heard from her again. Her remains were found in a chemical drum in a rented storage facility in 2000.

Sheila and Debbie Faith (1994): Forty-five-year-old Sheila, a struggling single mother, had a fifteen-year-old daughter named Debbie Faith who suffered from spina bifida, relegating the teen to a wheelchair. Robinson offered to pay Debbie's medical expenses and give Sheila a job. In 1994, the mother and daughter moved from Fullerton, California, to Kansas City and immediately disappeared. Robinson cashed Faith's pension checks for the next seven years. Their remains were discovered alongside Beverly's in his rented storage facilities in 2000.

Izabela Lewicka (1999): Active in BDSM chat rooms online, Robinson met twenty-one-year-old Polish native Izabela, who was living in Indiana in 1999. The basis of their sexual relationship was BDSM. When she moved to Kansas City, Missouri, Robinson gave Lewicka an engagement ring despite him still being married; she signed a 115-item slave contract that gave Robinson almost total control over every aspect of her life. Then she disappeared. Her body was found in a chemical barrel on Robinson's farm in Kansas in 2000.

Suzette Trouten (2000): A twenty-seven-year-old licensed practical nurse, Suzette Trouten moved from Michigan to

Kansas to travel with Robinson as his submissive sex slave. Later, Robinson told Trouten's mother that she had run off with an acquaintance after stealing money from him. Suzette's body was found in an oil drum on Robinson's farm in Kansas that same year.

Due to Robinson's methods of manipulation and the difficulty in identifying all his online interactions, authorities suspect that there might be other victims whose identities remain unknown.

TODAY

Octogenarian John Robinson remains on death row, in isolation twenty-three hours a day, at the El Dorado Correctional Facility in Kansas, despite also receiving multiple life sentences in bordering Missouri.

THE MEDIA

Anyone You Want Me to Be: A True Story of Sex and Death on the Internet (2004) by noted criminal profiler John Douglas and journalist Stephen Singular tracked the new dangers of a serial killer lurking on the internet in this bestselling true crime account of the case.

There have been countless television specials on the case: "Internet Slave Master," Dark Documentary series (2011); "Sole Survivor," *20/20* (2019); *The Internet's First Serial Killer: John E. Robinson*, BuzzFeed Unsolved Network (2020); "The Deranged

Case of Serial Killer John Robinson," *Cold Case Files*, A&E (2023); *Kidnapped by a Killer: The Heather Robinson Story*, Lifetime (2025)

LEFT BEHIND

One kidnapped adopted niece, Heather Tiffany Robinson

CHAPTER 4

WHEN "UNCLE JOHN" IS YOUR MOTHER'S KILLER

LEFT BEHIND: NIECE HEATHER TIFFANY ROBINSON

> If your looking for a good MASTER, write him . . . He is a great MASTER . . . emailaddy eruditemaster@email.com . . .
>
> —posting by John Edward Robinson online, giving himself a glowing reference

In a family photo "Uncle John" Robinson holds baby Heather on his knee, grinning . . . Only he knew the baby hadn't been legally adopted. Only he knew the adoption "fee" he took from his brother and sister-in-law did not go to attorneys. Only he knew that Heather's biological father, Carl Stasi, was alive and well, and there was a family failing to convince law enforcement that Lisa, while in a troubled situation, would not have run off to start a new life, not with a four-month-old infant. Was it a day after, hours after Uncle John had bludgeoned her mother with a hammer that he sat with baby Heather jovially for her first family photo?

Heather was too young to attend the trial. She did not sit in the courtroom, testify, or hear testimonies. Being shielded from the story imprisoned her with questions and galvanized her to come forward in adulthood as the "missing endangered infant" from 1985.

I knew Heather's story was different, but it wasn't until I sat down to write did I grasp the depth and breadth of that difference. So many things had been coming at Heather, major events that require superhuman strength to endure: the murder of your mother whom you were too small to remember; your own kidnapping; the bombshell that your uncle John was a serial killer who murdered her; the question of your adopted family's role; fighting to uphold the love you have for your adopted father—his brother—who raised you; a second family full of dysfunction, legal actions, and lawsuits—three lawsuits to be exact. Criminal, civil, and adoption lawsuits that add flavors of sourness and bitterness to Heather's already unsavory plight, except with each pour, she sticks her cup out for more and more servings.

Being related to a con artist can lead to two outcomes: either you learn the art of the con yourself, or you become obsessed with Truth. Heather Tiffany Robinson's "Uncle John" was a swindler, serial killer, her kidnapper, and the man who murdered her mother. Better believe she has a nose for bullshit.

If I could describe Heather in one phrase, it would be "say what you mean, mean what you say." She grew up in America's Midwest, in a suburb of Chicago, Illinois, known for its wholesome politeness. But she doesn't act on pretense. No "bless your hearts" when she really means "go to hell." She won't compliment you on your botched haircut or say yes to covering your weekend shift; she'll tell you to ask someone else. Whether you like it or not, whether she knows you or not, Heather gives you back what she gets. You cross her or push her or otherwise try to convince her to do something she doesn't want to, well, she'll—as Heather warns—"be done with you. And when I'm done, I'm done."

When I contacted Heather for this book, it was after her episode on *20/20* aired, and around the time when she was deciding whether to confront her uncle John about his secret life, specifically the 1985 murder of her biological mother, nineteen-year-old Lisa Stasi. As I helped her prepare the arrangements for a meeting with John Robinson, who is on death row, Heather's burning question to him is not "why?" But "where?"

Where's my mother's body, you piece of shit?

THE KIDNAPPING: TIFFANY STASI BECOMES HEATHER TIFFANY ROBINSON

John's wife Nancy Robinson testified that in early January 1985, "the day of the terrible snowstorm," Robinson brought a baby to their home in Stanley, Kansas, court records show. Robinson said that the baby's name was Tiffany and that he received her through a private adoption for his brother and sister-in-law, Donald and Helen Robinson. Robinson called Donald and Helen and told them a baby was available immediately. He said the birth mother had decided against adoption immediately after delivery, but the family did not support her decision, so she left the baby at a shelter and committed suicide.

Authorities say that in 1985, John Robinson met Lisa Stasi (born Lisa Elledge), a new mother at Hope House, a shelter for abused wives. She was separated from her husband, Carl, who reenlisted in the military and relocated. Lisa was only a teen herself, and John told her he could get her into a job training program in Texas, according to court records. John Robinson's modus operandi was to target vulnerable women having problems in their lives. With an abusive husband, an infant, and no money, Lisa was perfect.

Lisa agreed to meet Robinson at the Rodeway Inn in Overland Park, Kansas, in January 1985, and she took her four-month-old baby daughter, Tiffany, with her. Lisa was never seen again, and her body was never found. Authorities posit that John killed her a day shy of handing over the baby, Tiffany Stasi, to his brother and sister-in-law.

The court records state that Lisa Stasi "was 18 years old when she began dating Carl Stasi sometime after June 1983. Lisa married Carl in August 1984. She was pregnant at the time. On September 3, 1984, Lisa Stasi gave birth to her first child, Tiffany Lynn, at Truman Medical Center in Kansas City, Missouri. After Tiffany's birth, Stasi's marriage crumbled, and Carl reenlisted in the Navy. He reported for duty at Great Lakes Naval Base, outside Chicago, Illinois, in early January 1985."

Around the time Stasi began dating Carl, the court records say, John Robinson was looking for a private adoption opportunity for his younger brother, Donald Robinson, and Donald's wife, Helen, who lived in the Chicago area. At a family reunion in 1983, Donald and Helen told Robinson they were pursuing a private adoption. The brothers were not close and their families didn't spend much time together, but when John told his brother he knew an adoption attorney and would handle the process for his younger brother, Don and Helen took his offer. In fall 1984, Robinson told Donald and Helen a baby would be available in October. At Robinson's direction, Donald sent him a $2,500 cashier's check payable to Robinson's shell business, Equi II, allegedly to cover adoption-related fees. Failing to produce a baby, Robinson told Don and Helen the birth mother had decided not to place the child for adoption, but he kept the money anyway.

In November 1984, Robinson contacted Karen Gaddis, a social worker at Truman Medical Center, and told her that he and several Johnson County businessmen had developed a program to provide housing, transportation, daycare, and job training for young mothers and their babies.

John Robinson was quoted as saying he needed referrals for Caucasian women because the program already had African-American participants and needed racial balance. He was looking for a white woman in her teens or early twenties, who had a newborn child, was struggling or disadvantaged, and had no family support or ties. According to court documents, in January 1985, Robinson told Gaddis another organization, Hope House, had referred a young lady to his program, and he had placed her at a motel in Kansas. Lisa Stasi's aunt, Karen Moore, testified that she had contacted Hope House and took Lisa Stasi to the organization just before January 1, 1985.

Family members last saw Stasi and Tiffany in early January 1985. "Carl Stasi's sister, Kathy Klingensmith, babysat Tiffany often. On January 8, Lisa Stasi dropped Tiffany off at Klingensmith's home and told her she had met a man named John Osborne, who was going to help her get a job and finish her GED. Stasi said she might even get to travel as part of the job training program," the court records say.

Around 4:30 PM, Stasi "called her mother-in-law, Betty Stasi, in a panic, crying and hysterical. Stasi said 'they' were claiming that Betty Stasi planned to take Tiffany away because Stasi was an unfit mother. Stasi's mother-in-law told her not to believe what 'they' were saying because it was not true. Stasi said 'they' wanted her to sign four blank sheets of paper. Betty Stasi told her not to sign anything. Stasi said, 'here they come,' and she hung up," according to the court records.

Lisa Stasi's family never saw her again. The baby was gone, too.

Donald and Helen Robinson flew to Kansas City on January 10, 1985, to meet John. John picked them up at the airport in the late afternoon and drove them to the offices of Equi II in Overland Park, not far from the Rodeway Inn, where they signed legal paperwork, including a Petition for Adoption. According to *State v. Robinson*, a 2015 Supreme Court of Kansas decision, after signing the documents, Donald gave Robinson another cashier's check in the amount of $3,000 payable to "Doug Wood," a fictitious attorney, allegedly for further adoption expenses. Donald and Helen named the four-month-old baby Heather Tiffany Robinson. The new family of three returned to Chicago the following day.

John Robinson's name surfaced early in the investigation, when Robinson's parole office Steve Haymes looked into Lisa's disappearance. On February 1, 1985, Overland Park detectives interviewed John Robinson, who told them he was starting a charitable organization to provide young mothers with job training, food, and housing. Robinson admitted he had placed Stasi at the Rodeway Inn as part of that program, the records say. "However, he said Stasi had recently come to his office to give him the motel key. Robinson said Stasi thanked him for the assistance and said she had made other arrangements. Robinson claimed that Stasi and Tiffany left with a young Caucasian male."

After John Robinson's arrest in 2000, Donald and Helen began to question the identity of Heather's birth mother. Law enforcement compared Heather's footprints to the known prints of Tiffany and found the prints matched. Heather Tiffany Robinson was Tiffany, Lisa Stasi's biological daughter.

Don and Helen Robinson testified at John Robinson's trial. The couple described to the court how they flew to Kansas City from their home in Chicago in January 1985 to pick up the baby. As the trial continued, Don and Helen claimed that John Robinson told them that the mother wanted to give the baby up for adoption. He spun an elaborate tale, according to their testimony, telling them that the mother killed herself after abandoning the child in a shelter. It wasn't true, of course. Don and Helen weren't charged with conspiracy because it was believed they were oblivious to John Robinson's true scheme. "We named her Heather Tiffany Robinson," Don Robinson testified, "because Tiffany was the name that my brother claimed the child's mother had given her . . . We wanted to keep that in some way."

According to Helen Robinson's testimony, the couple couldn't have children and felt it would take a long time to adopt through an agency or charity. At a family reunion, they mentioned to John Robinson their desire to find a private adoption, unwittingly sealing Lisa Stasi's and baby Tiffany's fate.

MISSING ENDANGERED

Online, there's a baby photo of Tiffany Stasi on a flyer fit for the back of a milk carton: *Missing Endangered*, it says. Heather found the 1985 advertisement of her former identity online after she overheard a phone call between John Robinson's son and her father, Don, dropping the bomb that John had been arrested. She had never seen that photo of herself, provided by an alternate, unknown family.

"I was playing Sims online with an acquaintance from high school," Heather said, describing her fluke of a discovery. "He was supposed to call, and we were going to talk, but that's when the phone rang and my dad answered at the same time I did."

But it wasn't her teenage friend. "So I just stayed on the phone, hit the mute button so no one would hear me, and listened," said Heather. "All I really remember was him saying that John was arrested and that it had something to do with John's 'involvement with Heather's mother.' I can't remember if he said anything about other women. I remember my dad. I could definitely hear how he was confused. I remember him asking if this was a joke. And that was before any police or FBI or anyone had contacted us. I went downstairs, got on the computer, went on Yahoo or AOL, and then started finding the articles."

Uncle John had lured some of his victims with promises of money and jobs and requests for sadomasochistic sex, the articles told her. In 2000, it all unraveled when authorities discovered the remains of two women stuffed inside two fifty-five-gallon barrels sitting out in the open on rural property near La Cygne, Kansas. A storage locker with the remains of three other women was searched next. However, none of those women was Lisa Stasi.

For the first time, Heather had a name for her biological mother but not a face. It wasn't the way she had anticipated searching for her biological mother, as more than 65 percent of adopted children choose to do. As the weeks passed, the internet would become an ominous photo album that Heather would turn the pages of to piece together who her mother once was, including what she looked like. "Before photos of Lisa were posted, I thought Paula Godfrey, John's first victim, was my mother," Heather said. "So the first time I ever saw images of Lisa, of the person I had wondered about all my life, was through the internet news feeds about the whereabouts of her body and these strangers who claimed to be my relatives."

Heather desperately tried to keep up with claims made by people who said they knew and loved her mother. Photos of a carefree and beautiful Southern girl popped up alongside interviews with a man who said he was Heather's biological father, a maternal grandmother who was pleading to meet her long-lost granddaughter, and personal accounts about what happened on the last day they all saw Lisa. The more she heard from these strangers claiming to be related to her, one thing became clear. "My mother's circumstances were shaped not only by John but the negative impacts in her life that led to her to fall prey to him," Heather wrote in an email she sent to me at 5:28 AM in late January 2023. She was in part referring to the role she believed her biological father, Carl Stasi, indirectly played in her mother's vulnerability and ultimate fate. "This played a huge contributing factor to what would fuel this lifelong investigation into her, and why to this day I still advocate for her," Heather wrote.

As Heather researched her biological family and met members of her extended family, including her half sister, her aunts, and Carl himself, she came to believe that Carl's treatment of Lisa and his absence from their lives contributed to the instability Lisa faced as a young mother. In

Heather's view, those circumstances left Lisa isolated and more exposed to danger. "He obviously didn't kill her," Heather said. "He put her in a vulnerable situation to be killed, so I can see blame on his end. He never took the title or role of father . . . This played a huge contributing factor to what would fuel this lifelong investigation into her and why to this day I still advocate for her."

Uncle John, now in custody, and Don and Helen briefly investigated as persons of interest, Heather was pulled out of high school and home-schooled, confined mostly to her room—the internet acting as both her portal and her prison. As a minor, her identity was not released, but locally, she was yet again stigmatized. "The kid that actually was supposed to call that night to play Sims with me, he told me not to talk to him anymore. His family didn't want him to end up in a dumpster or something if he went out with me and my dad. Since then, people have said far worse."

Say what you will about Heather, but when it comes to her dad, Don, she will bark at you like a guard dog if you attack his character. Don Robinson experienced some of the backlash that typically happens when a close relative is arrested for murder: guilty by association. This was unbearable for a dutiful daughter to witness. The last time Don saw his brother was when he testified at his trial. "They walked John right past him while my dad was still in the fucking witness stand. And then John shook his hand. And then there was a whole news thing about how they shook hands . . . My dad was so freaked out. He didn't know what to do. He was like, 'I'm just standing there. I didn't know where to go; no one got me. They just walked him past me and he reached his hand out. I didn't know what to do, so I just reached my hand down and I shook it.' I'm like 'It's okay, Dad . . .'

"Everything my dad did was made into a salacious headline at the time. If they saw him shake Uncle John's hand, it was a headline. Even the most mundane innocent thing could be turned into something if it made or sold something at the time, and it was very different twenty years ago; there weren't all the regulations and rules now in place, especially to protect minors. It was a free-for-all when it came to me . . . as a fifteen-year-old, I was pretty much exploited in every fricking possible way. I'd search the internet and find crime scene photos. I bought a bunch of stuff online merch dealers were selling, because back then if you just googled Heather Robinson, the only thing that would come up was a serial killer memorabilia website with my baby pictures and my full name, and I wasn't thrilled."

THE FALLOUT

From a young age, Heather has possessed a knowing, a sensitivity to a person's energy, and she learned to trust that instinct as she grew older—because the knowing has never failed her. Her sixth sense picked up "creepy vibes" emitted by her uncle John, her adopted father's older brother, and were later confirmed in the most grandiose fashion.

Knowing what she knows now, when she looks at the picture of him holding her on his knee when she was just four months old, she sees past his beaming eyes and open-mouthed sales pitch of a grin and sees only evil, the kind of evil that not only murders but refuses to disclose where his victims' bodies remain.

Like any young niece, Heather Robinson didn't know much about her uncle, beyond his place in the family tree, who his wife and kids were, and a vague idea that he was some kind of businessman. What she did know was that he said inappropriate things to her, some sexual, and made her feel uncomfortable. Which is why when Uncle John was arrested for serial murders, she said she wasn't surprised in the least, describing her reaction as, "Confirmation. Reassurance that I wasn't crazy that the off-putting feeling and that horrible vibe and energy around him was very real, and I wasn't making it up in my head."

What's inside Heather's head has been an ever-present theme

throughout her life's journey. From a young age, she shared with me, she struggled with depression and anxiety, flirting with suicidal ideation and mysterious anger. Mysterious, because the source of her anger wasn't obvious.

Heather knew as early as age six that she had been adopted by Helen and Don Robinson, John Robinson's younger brother. Her middle name, Tiffany, she knew was an homage to her birth mother who had chosen that name as Heather's birth name. Don and Helen were a loving couple who had desperately wanted a child but couldn't conceive one. Her doting adopted father, Don, the head of household and breadwinner, went off to work every day leaving his wife, Helen, with baby Heather in a more traditional arrangement, as a stay-at-home mother. Don had a solid job in retail management. The family had three cats. Her home was clean and comfortable. Heather had her own computer with a dial-up AOL account and listened to New World Order. Her bedroom walls were covered with posters of *Home Improvement*'s Jonathan Taylor Thomas and the movie *Titanic*. But inside her middle-class existence, Heather acted out.

"At a very early age I always knew I needed to find my mom," Heather wrote in the same January email. Through our extensive Zoom interviews, I discovered Heather had kept journals when she was younger, writing to express her inner turmoil. I sensed maybe she'd like to respond to some of my questions in writing, and based on her beautifully insightful prose, it looked like I was right.

Her email continued, "At different variations of my life I needed to know my mother for different reasons. As a little girl, I longed for my mommy, dreaming that she was the missing piece that would make me feel whole and complete. Growing into a very hormonal, confused teenage girl, I was curious about who she was. Were we similar? Was I like her? Would she have liked me?

"As I got older and should have started to mature and grow, trauma stunted me in this weird place between traumatized teenage girl and adulthood. Some days I needed my mommy, others I needed to know who she was as a woman."

Perhaps doctors didn't know this or consider it once Heather began to exhibit emotional issues, which started in her adolescence. Heather described her early teen years as being isolating, having few friends and getting along better with boys than girls. By the time Heather was in high school, her main source of socialization was the internet, the same world in which her uncle John infamously and sinisterly did his deeds.

"As a teenager, I was in my own private little hell," Heather told me, recollecting her numerous hospitalizations in mental facilities. "Mixed with learning disabilities in school and not knowing how to deal with that, I got hospitalized a lot, some of it my own doing. When I was younger, I had a lot of fire and fight in me. I didn't take it from anyone. And it didn't matter who you were and what 'title' you thought you had, you weren't gonna talk to me in a certain way. So, I think it was just easier for the school to remove me than to deal with me."

The title of "mother" didn't carry much weight for Heather either, leading Helen and Heather to have some fierce blowouts. "I fought her adamantly," she said.

This was well before the truth about Lisa Stasi's murder came out. And before authorities theorized that Heather was a four-month-old witness present in the same room as her mother at the Rodeway Inn, where John Robinson likely bludgeoned Lisa to death with a hammer and stole little Heather, then Tiffany Stasi. If the doctors would've known this, would they have diagnosed Heather's behaviors as symptoms of trauma? It is believed by many professionals that trauma—even experienced before memory forms—can be ingrained on a cellular level. Instead, Heather said, the interventions did more harm than good.

"When hospitalized, I was put with children who were raped and sodomized by family members. It was there that I was introduced to self-harm. I had never thought of cutting myself until I learned that in the hospital. I learned a lot of stupid things that I ended up doing as a form of coping, surviving.

"I could show the signs and symptoms of ADHD, but I also exhibited the signs of bipolar, and then exhibited the signs of this, this, and this, and no one could quite figure me out and understand. And with me being adopted, they had no medical history to go off. So they just kind of guessed what was wrong with me. But when you tried to treat me with the traditional treatments of one diagnosis, it just didn't work. I did not react to lithium like most people with bipolar do. It nearly killed me. I started having organ issues and lost weight. I didn't become sedated or zombified from Ritalin. Instead, I flipped the fuck out and started breaking shit and going absolutely crazy and had no self-control. I don't even know anymore what actions were of my doing or the medications'. Especially now, twenty and thirty years later, seeing how many children have done really dumb things that they may not have done had they not been on medication they probably shouldn't have been prescribed."

As Heather struggled with her unnamed plight, in and out of hospitals, isolating herself further from Helen, succumbing to a black hole of loneliness and depression, without explanation, Uncle John had continued to lure, capture, rape, and kill eight known victims.

In 2000, when the news broke about who her uncle John was and his role in Heather's abduction, Heather was stigmatized for being "the girl at school who needed meds" and singled out for her murderous uncle. The suicide ideation returned. Now caught between three families—the Stasi family; Lisa's family, the Elledges; and the Robinsons—Heather felt more alone and confused and angry than ever. There were few outlets for processing, and the matter of her being the victim of a kidnapping seemed to render her without an identity, an outsider. A Stasi, an Elledge, or a Robinson? The niece of a serial killer or the daughter of a murder victim? A kidnapped victim herself? "That outsider shit," she said, "was an understatement.

"Most people thought I was either going to be murdered, kill myself, or become a drug addict," Heather said. "I'm almost forty, and I still hear shit from people. They can't believe that I thrive and that I overcame shit."

In documenting the experiences of the families in this book, the focus on emotions and shock and stigma, the bad behaviors of the media, and self-blame abound. In Heather's case, she has witnessed the suffering of both victims' and perpetrators' families—belonging to each in different ways—while also coming to terms with her own kidnapping. This has led her to search not for meaning or acceptance but for a need to confront herself, wholeheartedly choosing her identity. A Robinson or a Stasi? But the identity is not only a question of family ties; it is in the amorphous space between being the family member of a perpetrator and a family member of a victim. Possessing both roles is why Heather's experience is the outlier in this book.

"John is a monster but he was never my monster. He isn't the boogie man that keeps me up at night, he isn't this missed lost uncle or anything of substantial value. He's a part of a puzzle I've been collecting pieces to for decades," Heather's email said. "There is no confrontation, no tears of pleas or hoping with time he'll come to compassion and understanding to the victims and families. Who I am naturally as a person correlates with how and why I've spent my life looking into every aspect of everything related to this. Life, circumstances, growth, determination, and refusal to back down, even if it breaks me, are what brought me here."

A minor when the arrest and trial happened, Heather has not seen nor spoken to Uncle John, who has been in jail for going on three decades, and who has not divulged the location of her mother's body. To be the person who guides her mother Lisa Stasi to her final resting place, Heather believes she can finally create new meaning in her life and manifest her mother's meaning, too.

MY NAME IS HEATHER ROBINSON

Heather has an uncanny ability to articulate all that she's lost without one ounce of victimhood. Not all of her life has been about voids. While longing for her mother as a child, she relished the one gift that had been given to her—a gift I never had—a loving, proud father.

"I already have a dad. I don't need another one," Heather said in response to the question about whether she had a relationship with her biological father, Carl Stasi, whom she said she had never wondered about growing up. Even when Carl demanded to meet Heather, once he knew she was alive, Heather said she "wasn't interested in a family reunion." Later in adulthood, she did agree to meet with him, but they do not share a relationship today.

Heather's bond with her adopted father is enough. Their kindred relationship began the moment Don and his wife signed fake adoption papers. "I always felt very comfortable and safe with my dad," Heather said as she remembers her childhood with Don. "He understands why I do the things I do. And he supports me a hundred percent as I continue to find the answers for Lisa. And that man never looked at me differently or made me feel like I wasn't still just Heather. And that was something that I have not experienced with many people."

Heather shared a letter her father Don Robinson wrote to Carl Stasi in 2000 on Heather's behalf when she was sixteen and struggling with her mental health, coming to grips with the truth about her past. Once she knew the truth about how she came to be Heather Robinson, Heather became more confused and depressed, revisiting her ideation with suicide; her questions and confusion plagued her. In an effort to assuage his daughter's pain and give her some semblance of control and understanding of who her mother was, while also collecting her biological family's mental health history for doctors, Don would do anything to fight for his daughter's peace.

Being Daddy's Girl is the silver lining in this tragic story. Heather's voice danced when she talked about Don, a rare lightheartedness in our otherwise heavy series of interviews, especially ones about her biological father. "I never had an interest in having a relationship with Carl Stasi," she said with blunt force, in answer to the question, "Did you ever consider changing your name back to Tiffany Stasi?"

"I was Tiffany for four months; Heather for fifteen years," she continued. "John did tell the Robinsons that my name was Tiffany. He did not lie about that. He would tell truth with lies. Looking at his letters and his artwork, within the lies there's a shred of truth. He said I was born on October twelfth, and I was Lithuanian. But I was born on September third, and I'm not Lithuanian. But my name is Tiffany.

"My dad has always been in my corner. For a very long time, my dad was my best friend. We just naturally clicked. My dad was just kind of the rock and foundation that tried his damnedest to keep everything together."

Today Don Robinson lives a minute up the road from his only daughter, Heather.

THE LISA STASI EFFECT: CONFRONTATION AND COMMUNITY

When you break through the barrier of silence and tell your story, it can be impactful. And for a truth teller and seeker like Heather, it's hard to stop demanding answers once you've started. John Robinson retained an attorney to appeal his two life sentences. If granted, Robinson would be allowed in general population, a 180-degree turn from his twenty-three hours a day in death-row isolation. So far, Robinson's appeals have largely failed: the Kansas Supreme Court maintained his death sentence, and the US Supreme Court passed on reviewing the case. His most recent appeals in 2022 also did not yield a new trial or sentencing change. In short—no major legal changes or reprieves so far.

I play back the scene of visiting my father in a prison visiting room with my young children and see what I was looking for is nothing like what Heather wants to achieve if she gets to see Uncle John. She's older than I was at the time, and she is wiser to the ways of sociopaths than my younger self. She, for instance, knows the best lies contain a hint of truth. I had wanted to see if a father can be separated from a serial killer. Heather wants to prove what she already knows: her uncle's face is only a shell for resident evil, and he lives on power, trying to exude it over her and Lisa Stasi to this very day.

"It would be fantastic if he was at a place where he was willing to offer answers and closure. I just don't suspect that to be a likely scenario based on experience and information obtained," Heather said, her instincts still aptly protecting her from the underpinnings of false hope.

"I have spoken to anyone and everyone who would talk to me about this that was involved—from family to law enforcement. Over the years with the development of my Facebook group, 'The Lisa Stasi Effect,' I've received potential tips on the whereabouts of my mom's body. Anyone who ever knew her can find me here, to tell me about her, to help me piece together my own clues. All that aside there are a multitude of reasons why a face-to-face is warranted with John. From my right as a victim, family member, and Lisa's advocate. It may come off entitled, but isn't part of the justice for those impacted by crimes to be able to face the person if they chose to? I didn't attend the trial; I didn't see him charged."

The evidentiary hurdles are substantial: unlike Robinson's later victims (whose remains were discovered in barrels in Kansas and Missouri), Lisa's body was never located. Without it, prosecutors lacked forensic evidence (such as DNA or cause of death) to build a direct murder case. "Google told me about the technicalities against John that changed the status of the outcome with Lisa," Heather wrote. "So are Lisa and I even legally victims anymore? Would new information and evidence, including my mother's body, open the door to new charges?"

At the time of this writing, Heather has reached out via letter to

John's defense attorney, asking for a meeting. So far, there's been no response.

"There are a lot of questions that remain, and maybe I'm just stubborn, but I refuse to let that man keep all the power. There must be others—law enforcement, witnesses, detectives—who not only can figure out where my mother's remains are, but what her last hours were like, how long I remained in the room with her as a baby before he swept me up and sold me off. Was it quick and painless or did she suffer? Did I cry? Did my senses heighten even in infanthood to the loss of the closest being to me?

"And until someone else starts asking these questions, talking to these people, looking into this information, I'll continue to do it myself."

CASE #4

DREW PETERSON, KILLER COP

THE CRIME

Retired Midwestern police sergeant Drew Peterson came to the nation's attention in the fall of 2007 when his wife Stacy simply vanished in suburban Illinois. Twenty-three-year-old Stacy Ann Cales Peterson was one-third her husband's age, his fourth wife, mother to Drew's two youngest children, and by all accounts deeply unhappy with her living situation. Drew Peterson had been the last person to see his wife. Despite his brazen insistence that his much younger spouse craved male attention and had run off with another man, he quickly became the only suspect.

Stacy's inexplicable disappearance reignited interest in the mysterious death of Drew's third wife, Kathleen Savio, three years earlier. Her death three months after an acrimonious divorce from Drew—her nude body had been found in a dry bathtub with a deep gash to the head—had officially been ruled an accident. Drew had an alibi: he had been with his new wife in their house just up the street from Savio's, and Stacy fully supported him.

In 2007 Stacy did not return, prompting police to reopen the investigation into Kathleen's death, and her body was exhumed for tests. In 2008 her death was officially reclassified as a homicide, and a year later Drew Peterson was arrested and charged with her murder. He hired a "dream team" of six sunglasses-wearing attorneys who cracked jokes at press conferences and were confident they could get their client off due to the lack of physical evidence.

After some extremely damaging testimony from several witnesses blew up their defense case in front of their eyes, even Drew's son Tom's support for his father on the stand meant very little. In 2012, Drew Peterson was found guilty of murder in the first degree of Tom's mother, Kathleen Savio, and sentenced to thirty-eight years in prison. Peterson threw an angry fit in court, claiming he had been railroaded.

Remanded to prison and held in a special area away from the general population, Peterson's story wasn't over yet. He appealed his conviction, claiming he'd had ineffective counsel. Though one of his six previous lawyers took this appeal on, it was turned down. In 2015, Peterson was charged again with solicitation of murder-for-hire for having tried to hire a hit man to take out James Glasgow, the Illinois state prosecutor who had had put him away. Wiretaps helped to seal his fate. For his latest crime, Peterson was convicted and sentenced to serve an additional forty years.

THE VICTIMS

Kathleen Savio (2004): Forty-one, third wife of Drew Peterson, mother of two of his sons.

Stacy Ann Cales (missing/presumed dead, 2007): Twenty-three, fourth wife of Drew Peterson, mother to two of his children. To this day her body has not been found.

TODAY

After being held in a federal facility in Terre Haute, Indiana, in connection with a murder-for-hire charge, in December 2019 Peterson's location was once again changed, this time to an undisclosed out-of-state facility.

THE MEDIA

The case of a pretty young wife of a cop whose previous wife had died under suspicious circumstances vanishing into thin air was true crime catnip for readers and online sleuths everywhere.

"Did He Kill Two Wives?" asked *People* magazine in December 2007, publishing cover shots of both women and one of Drew in uniform, smirking.

Fatal Vows: The Tragic Wives of Sergeant Drew Peterson by journalist Joseph Hosey, who had covered the case in Illinois, was released in 2008.

Rob Lowe played Drew Peterson in Lifetime's 2012 movie *Drew Peterson: Untouchable.*

Peterson's sons Tom and Steve appeared together to discuss their new lives on *Dr. Oz Crimewatch*.

In 2017, Steve was confronted by Kathleen Savio's sister, Sue Doman, on an episode of *Monster in My Family* on A&E, where I moderated their meeting in hopes they would find common ground and compassion for each other's traumatic losses and experiences.

LEFT BEHIND

Stephen Peterson, whose life changed forever in the wake of his father's murder conviction in 2012. Many people in his community and across the nation went as far as accusing Steve of having some involvement with Stacy's disappearance, claiming "the apple doesn't fall far from the tree."

CHAPTER 5

WHEN A SON PAYS FOR THE SINS OF THE FATHER

LEFT BEHIND: SON STEPHEN PETERSON

The ultimate measure of a man is not where he stands in moments of comfort and convenience, but where he stands at times of challenge and controversy.

—Martin Luther King Jr.

Stephen Peterson threw me off. Not because he was scary or violent or even mean—but because he reflected too much of me back at myself. When I was first scheduled to meet Steve, as he is called by friends and family, it was in 2017 for the first episode of Season 2 of *Monster in My Family.* I took a deep dive into his complex story, one so layered, you could lose yourself in the folds of a family saga beyond the loss of one woman's life. I felt an instant kinship with Steve, a camaraderie, because I found many parallels in our experiences. Many things he said sparked in me a memory, an insight, a feeling that I'd blurt out with emphasis, because I can count on a few fingers the number of people who mirror my adult life path as closely as Steve does.

Steve's kind voice has a beat of calm in it, with dropped vowels that signal he comes from a city near the Great Lakes. The incorporated village of Bolingbrook, where he still lives, twenty-eight miles southwest of Chicago, boasts the motto "A Place to Grow." Steve's growth in the face of tragedy tells much about his character and about how differently people react to the trauma of having a killer dad.

Steve was born the same year I was, and he is the only other person in this book who grew up with a parent who, while raising children, was secretly taking lives. He is the second oldest of six children, four of whom are his half-siblings. I am the oldest of four kids, one who is the product of my mother's second marriage to a wife beater. Domestic violence is a through line in the Peterson case, with photos of victim Kathleen Savio wearing bruises on her eyes and body. My mother was also a victim of domestic violence, my stepfather battering her body and bruising all of our spirits for years.

The similarities between Steve and me continue. I learned how Drew manipulated and tried to control Steve and his siblings from inside prison. Steve shared with me letters from his father telling him how much he loved him and that the only thing "keeping me sane in here is knowing you and the kids are all alright."

Like Steve, my father to this day continues to try to let me know that he is keeping tabs on me, with informants on the outside reporting to him details of my personal and professional life. One letter a few years ago commented on my physical appearance: "You gained weight, Missy," he wrote. He was talking about how I looked in my wedding dress, the subliminal message being, *I know what you are up to, even when you don't tell me.* "How come I wasn't invited to the wedding?" he wrote in another letter, his sarcasm sickening my stomach.

It wasn't uncommon for Drew to call Steve a few times a week, with the guise of checking on the kids, but then turning into requests for favors. Drew would ask Steve to contact people on his behalf, transfer funds, relay messages to the kids, as if Steve were merely an errand boy rather than the son who stepped up to raise his siblings. He also received passive-aggressive letters that seemed to have an ulterior motive of controlling his kids, in particular their support of his innocence, from the inside.

What I related to most was how Steve seemed to deal with the pain. Just like me, he used dark humor when our discussions broached sensitive subjects.

I found one difference between Steve and me. At first, he had believed in his father's innocence. Steve was close with his father and had a blind trust in his word. This resulted in a much slower acceptance of his father's guilt. On the other hand, I had known on some level that my father was demented and capable of his serial killing. Steve's journey is one of a slow corrosion of his perception of his father.

My father not only confessed he was the Happy Face Killer, he did so with hubris. Drew, on the other hand, sticks to his story that Kathleen's death was an accident and that Stacy had a Mommy Makeover and ran off to live her best life. Without their father's admission of guilt, the kids would never be 100 percent convinced their father was the monster the jury had found him to be. Which made it difficult for Steve to stop taking his dad's calls and say no to his father's every request—at first.

When Drew was first arrested, he asked Steve to watch over the kids. He asked him to hold on to his rifles for him before police swept every room looking for evidence. Naively believing his father would never implicate his son or drag him into his mess, Steve agreed, opening up allegations that he was keeping his father's secrets and perhaps should also be a suspect. Because of Steve's compliance with Drew's request, Steve was fired from the Oak Brook Police Department, where he worked as a police officer.

"I just never thought he'd do that to me, get me in trouble like that,"

Steve told me when I visited him at his Bolingbrook home, once owned by Drew.

After his father's arrest, Steve's marriage fell apart. "My wife and I had built a beautiful new house together and took vacations to the west coast of Mexico and the Caribbean or Aruba three or four times a year. Nothing was holding us back. Then the world came crashing down," he said.

No longer employed, Steve went broke. He moved into his father's home in Bolingbrook to be a surrogate dad to his four motherless half siblings, while being a new father of his own baby. After news of Stacy's disappearance and the reexamination of Kathleen's death, the pleasant suburban home on Pheasant Chase Court became the site of a media onslaught. Crowds of reporters forced the traumatized children, all under the age of fourteen, to climb out a window just to go to school. Because he didn't say no to his father's requests or question his motives, Steve's marriage, career, future, and identity were zapped out of existence. These are the unsurprising aftershocks of being the son of a murderer. These are the things that happen when you love your father, trust his word, and fight for his defense.

"At the time, in my mind, there was no way I could think my dad could murder," Steve explained, "so I didn't think anything of doing what he asked. I felt like, he's a cop and my dad. He isn't capable of this."

Denial becomes the shadow of gaslighting when there's a killer in the family.

While all of Drew Peterson's children recall their father being a present, doting, and active participant in their day-to-day lives, Drew Peterson had an extensive and complicated marital history. He was a man who craved female company . . . whether or not he was currently married. It seemed he traded in his wife for a younger model, and he did so three times, producing six children with a total of four wives.

The son of a Marine who was a strict disciplinarian, Drew was a high school athlete who served in the Army. His first marriage to high school sweetheart Carol produced two sons, Eric and Stephen. They appeared to be a picture-perfect family, with the young cop and father named Officer of the Year. But it was not to be: their six-year marriage ended in 1980, with Drew's infidelities a major source of friction. Peterson became briefly engaged to twenty-year-old Kyle Piry, who met Officer Peterson on the job as he was investigating a crime at the gas station where she worked. A sign of things to come.

After Piry broke the engagement, Peterson would go on to marry twenty-three-year-old single mom Victoria Rutkiewicz in 1982; the couple divorced ten years later in 1992. Vicki later spoke publicly (including to the *Chicago Tribune* and during TV interviews), saying Drew was controlling, manipulative, and abusive during their marriage. Drew met twenty-eight-year-old Kathleen Savio that same year on a blind date; the romance moved fast and the couple became engaged only six months later, even as he was settling his last divorce. Kathleen appeared to be very much in love; they settled down and Kathleen quickly had two sons, Matthew and Richard.

Stacy Cales first met Drew in 2001, when she was seventeen and working as a desk clerk at the local SpringHill Suites. There was a thirty-year age gap, an age difference that son Eric disapproved of to the point he stopped talking to his father entirely. Stacy's parents had split up in 1990, when she was about six. Her mother, Christine Toutges, had a history of depression and alcoholism, and her father, Anthony Cales, was awarded custody of Stacy and her two siblings, brother Yelton and sister Cassandra. The family moved around a lot, and Anthony remarried five years later. When she was in high school, Stacy went to live with her older half sister, Tina Kokas, Christine's daughter from a previous relationship.

Eerily Stacy's mother, Christine, disappeared in March 1998, when Stacy was fourteen. According to reports, she had left her house with her purse and Bible, possibly on her way to church or to a friend's house, and was never seen again. Nobody has any further information on this mystery.

Within weeks of meeting Stacy in 2001, Drew installed her in the basement of his family's home, unbeknownst to Kathleen and their two sons, Mathew and Richard. An anonymous note—presumably from someone who worked with her husband—eventually tipped Kathleen off to her husband's affair. It let her know that Drew's behavior had become "an ongoing joke within the department." Kathleen filed for divorce and the split was finalized in October 2003, but animosity lingered. Kathleen didn't want to let the proceedings go without the assets she felt were owed her after their eleven-year marriage, which had ended in a most humiliating fashion.

Drew wasted no time remarrying, tying the knot with Stacy on October 18, 2003, the ink on his divorce barely dry and just shy of three months after they welcomed son Anthony. Daughter Lacy (named after Stacy's little sister who died in infancy) was born in 2005. In 2006, Stacy's older sister Tina died of cancer, and not long afterward, friends and family got the impression that this was a game changer. Something in Stacy had shifted. After Lacy was born, the young mom had undergone a tummy tuck and a breast enhancement and had gotten braces. Preparing for a new life, a fresh start?

Kathleen left behind the two young sons, Mathew and Richard, as well as a life insurance policy, which, despite their divorce, still named former husband Drew Peterson as beneficiary. As soon as the ink was dry on Kathleen's death certificate, Drew had his current fourth wife, Stacy, adopt both boys. "When you adopt children," Steve explained, "the children are issued entirely new birth certificates, which replaces the birth parents' names with the adoptive ones. So now Kathy's no longer on the birth certificates, and it's Stacy who is named their mother. If you look at the date of the births, Stacy would've been like nine years old when they were born."

Three years later, when Drew's current wife, twenty-three-year-old Stacy Peterson, disappeared, investigators decided to take another look at what happened to Kathleen. After they exhumed her body, Kathleen's death was redesignated a homicide. A number of facts the inquest jury never heard back in 2004 when Kathleen's death was ruled accidental—a slip and fall while taking a shower—now came to light. Most prominent among them included records of eighteen police home visits for domestic disturbance calls.

Despite the calls and Kathleen's attempts at getting a restraining order against her estranged husband in 2002, Drew was never once taken into custody. In November 2002, Kathleen had written to Will County Assistant State's Attorney Elizabeth Fragale, saying with urgency, "He knows how to manipulate the system, and his next step is to take my children away. Or kill me instead." Her worst fears would be manifested. At the time of Kathleen's failed plea to the state attorney, Drew, forty-seven, had already been caught having an affair with seventeen-year-old Stacy Cales.

A few days before *she* disappeared, Stacy Peterson told divorce attorney Harry Smith that she knew her husband had killed Kathleen, and she was thinking of leaving him. Stacy wanted to take all four kids with her—Anthony and Lacy, as well as Matt and Rich, whom Stacy had grown close to (especially after they moved in full time after their mother died).

THE VANISHING

Drew Peterson said that on the morning of Sunday, October 28, 2007, he had awoken at 11 AM to find his wife of four years, twenty-three-year-old Stacy Peterson, already gone for the day—off to help paint at a friend's house. Stacy did not return home.

Stacy's sister Cassandra Cales, having been unable to reach Stacy all that day, went to the Peterson home on Pheasant Chase Court at 11 PM that night. Neither Drew nor Stacy was there, and one of the children told her they had had a big fight that morning. Cassandra called the Illinois State Police to report her sister missing at 4 AM on Monday.

This was major news in Bolingbrook. On October 29, Stacy's aunt Suzan Robison told a local paper that two days before she disappeared, Stacy had told Drew she wanted a divorce. He was "a very jealous, very controlling person," Robison said. "He followed her. He tracked her with GPS on her cell phone, called her constantly."

Every resource the authorities had was dispatched, from tracker dogs to divers, but no trace of Stacy could be found. The same day state police called her case a "potential homicide," less than two weeks after she disappeared, the Will County state's attorney's office officially reopened the investigation into Kathleen's 2004 death and had her body exhumed.

Stacy's family, meanwhile, was appalled at how Peterson—who had already been suspended from the Bolingbrook Police Department in September 2007 for an alleged "serious lack of judgment" during a police pursuit and then resigned November 20 with his full $6,068 monthly pension—was behaving in light of everything that was happening. Too nonchalant, they felt. Like it was just another wife gone . . . no big deal.

LITTLE BOY BLUE BLOOD

Having a killer in the family pits your brain against your heart in a dead-end debate. The brain asks, *Is my loved one a monster?* The heart asks, *Or did he perform monstrous acts?* For some, the two are mutually exclusive. For others, there is no difference. But there is a middle ground, a purgatory of grappling between what your brain knows to be true and the memories of love and attention that make even the hardest evidence questionable. When children have parents who kill, positive childhood memories can become temptations to rationalize: *My father can murder in cold blood but still have a warm heart. Can't he? He may have hated his victim, but he loves me. Right?*

For Steve, whatever evidence pointed to in terms of his father's guilt, he couldn't undo the years of a father-son relationship worthy of a greeting card. Steve followed in his father's footsteps and became a cop. He idolized his macho father, who had spent time undercover as a narcotics detective. "He had a whole different name, a whole different persona to hold up," Steve explained, walking me through the behind-the-scenes of police life. "The joke back in the day was you had to lie to your girlfriends to get home to your wife. Dad was very deep into it. John Wilson is what they called him. I have his ID somewhere. He had long hair that made him look like a hippie.

"When you're a kid, having a cop dad is awesome," Steve told me, sounding like a kid himself. "He'd take us on ride-alongs and let us do the radar. I remember when I told my dad I was switching my major from graphic art to criminal justice, he was very excited. After that, knowing that I would become a cop like him, we began to have more in common and we bonded."

Drew jumped at the opportunity to become his son's mentor and personal tutor. "Dad was a training officer, so every minute was a teaching moment," said Steve, who still feels a bitterness toward the brass who accused him of colluding with Drew in the murder of Kathleen. "After I graduated, I had about twenty thousand dollars in student loans and my dad just cut me a check right there. So, it was definitely a huge relief to be able to start life after college debt-free."

Remembering his father's generosity, both monetary and emotional, made our discussion of whether Steve thought his father purposely implicated him in his crimes difficult to process. With no cause for concern of the fallout Steve might experience, Drew asked him for a few favors that would change the course of Steve's life forever. I realized this would be another difference between my father and Steve's. My dad hadn't tried to take me down with him.

Having a killer in the family increases the likelihood of you becoming a suspect.

"At the end of October 2007, I think it was a Sunday night, my father called me and said Stacy had left him for another man and that she took twenty-five grand out of the account, the title to the car, and in Illinois, ran off with a boyfriend," Steve said, as he began to recount the slow burn of manipulation he fell victim to. "It wasn't exactly a shock. She was younger than I was. I felt bad for him, but Stacy's sister wasn't buying any of it. Then, Tuesday morning, I was lying in bed and my buddy called me and asked, 'Is that your dad on TV?' I turned the TV on and there it was, 'Missing Bolingbrook Mother,' and a picture of Stacy. I called my father and was like, 'What the hell?'"

Drew's response was cool and composed, as he described the media circus that had pitched a tent outside his house. It was likely difficult for Steve to imagine at the time, and he had no way of knowing how deeply this would affect the children living in the home, yet they were all on Steve's mind.

"I didn't question him," Steve remembered. "I felt bad for him because his wife left him. It didn't sink in that something foul was going on. I just put it in my mind that this will blow over sooner or later when Stacy comes back and people look stupid for being overly dramatic about a marriage that is splitting up. It could come that she left him for another guy, and it'd be over. I really just questioned him about the kids, to see if they were okay."

At this point, there was no reason to think Drew had a pattern of killing his wives. Remember, Kathleen's death had been ruled an accident, with nobody suspecting otherwise. "We became part of the daily news cycle. You couldn't turn on the TV without there being some kind of news story about the old man and a young missing fourth wife. Everybody wanted to be a part of it," Steve said. "The neighbor next door had a shrine on her lawn for Stacy with a sign pointing toward our house that said, 'Where's Stacy?' Every day, hearing interviews with strangers and acquaintances making up things that they 'saw' or 'heard,' all just to get some attention."

This is a common plight that families of perpetrators must contend with, beyond the shock and horror of having a loved one be a nefarious murderer: leeches and liars who want to insert themselves into the story for their fifteen minutes of fame. When the media gets involved, ordinary people who usually mean no harm get caught up in the spectacle. Pointing out the house or driving by to see it, they fail to take into consideration that there are innocent people inside, often children, peering through the blinds. People insert themselves into the narrative because they *think* they want to know how it feels. Anyone who actually lives through such a horror knows well enough that this is something you should *never* want to feel. It's not a role to play.

The news, social media, and armchair spectators see the crime only in one dimension. People with monsters in their family are well aware that behind the one-dimensional newspaper photo of the house, the newsreel of the yellow tape, the camera pan of the press conference on TV, there are innocent people—three-dimensional people—who will be affected forever.

Still believing his father's story, Steve was well aware that Drew would be a person of interest. In the case of murder, it's not uncommon for the spouse of the deceased to be the first questioned. Being that Drew was not only a cop but a sergeant, he was well aware of the procedures. Steve explained, "My father knew they'd come and search the house, so he came over to my house and said that he didn't want the police to mess around or mess up his guns. He had an expensive custom-built AR-15, a twenty-two, and a shotgun. 'Hold them for me,' my dad said."

Steve wasn't fazed by this request. "Now, if he had handed me a bloody knife or blade or something, of course I would've known. But, I mean, he's my dad, he wouldn't steer me wrong. He wouldn't get me involved in something I shouldn't be involved in." So Steve stored the guns at the house as his father had requested.

As if in prep mode, Drew took an equity line of credit against the house for $215,000. "He gives me a check," Steve said, the pace of his words speeding up, his voice less forgiving. "And he tells me, 'Here, if anything happens to me, use this to raise the kids.' I'm thinking, *What the heck is going to happen to you?*"

Steve didn't cash the check, but the situation became noticeably more serious. During the police search of Drew's home, they asked about the guns that were registered to him, which had not been uncovered in the search. Drew told the police his son had the guns for safekeeping.

Then, the Bolingbrook Police Department spent an hour interviewing Steve, putting him in the hot seat. The cops called around to interview Steve's friends and coworkers, trying to catch him in a lie. Steve offered to bring in his father's guns and did, but it didn't help his case. Usually the one watching the interrogation, Steve said, "I knew what all these tactics meant. I began to feel resentful of their hostile tactics, being a fellow police officer and them treating me like a criminal."

According to the Law Enforcement Officers Safety Act, police officers are permitted to own or have guns in their possession. What the grand jury seemed to be after was whether Steve had accepted hush money from his father, in the amount of $215,000—except that the money wasn't in Steve's account; he had returned it to his father. The grand jury let it drop, but Steve's chief of police didn't. "They took my star and my gun, claiming that I had impeded an investigation," he said.

Steve was shaken from the quiet slumber of his dream life. His name was now making headlines of its own; articles questioned his reputation and motives. Suddenly, he was the new "bad cop," with headlines insinuating that he had conspired with his father.

Despite the birth of Steve's first child in February 2009, the turbulence surrounding the case sent Steve's emotional stability into free fall. "It was open season on me," Steve said. "I had to hide who I was when my daughter was born, because we didn't want people at the hospital to know, and I began to see how our lives were never going to be completely normal."

At around the time Steve's daughter turned three months old, Drew was arrested, leaving Matt, Rich, Anthony, and Lacy, then approximately sixteen, fifteen, six, and four years old respectively, in need of a home and supervision. So, Steve and his wife went from having one newborn to five kids while awaiting Drew's trial, frequently checking on the vacant house until Drew's presumed acquittal.

"Things were stressful, and I didn't handle things the right way. We knew it [the arrest] was coming and thought we were ready, but you're never really mentally ready. I developed major anxiety. I couldn't leave the house without popping a Xanax. Depression set in. I drank a lot. I was numbing out. I was going out with the guys and doing the wrong things. My wife was a new mom at home with all my siblings. She would tell me I needed help; she tried to be there for me. I just pushed her away. I didn't want to hear it. To appease my wife, I went to a therapist once and told her what was going on, and she actually told me she didn't think she could help me, which was enough to signal me that I was too much for these people. One of my [former] coworkers knew I was running around on my wife and told me to get help. When someone on the outside is recognizing your behavior, it opens your eyes. It was a reckoning."

Under the weight of the upheaval of almost every aspect of the couple's life, the marriage fell apart. Before their daughter turned one, their divorce was final. Still believing his father was innocent and that the truth would eventually come to light, Steve moved himself and his siblings into his father's empty house in 2009. Jobless, wifeless, and fatherless, Steve and his siblings waited out the fate of their future in the house on Pheasant Chase Court. Steve did his best to provide the children with the guidance and support they needed, becoming their father in the absence of their own.

Drew Peterson was indicted and arrested for Kathleen's murder on May 7, 2009. Bail was set at $20 million, but while he was still wrestling with banks over home equity and other financial matters to post bond, a judge remanded him to jail for the duration of the trial.

At the murder trial, Drew's stepbrother Thomas Morphey testified that he had helped Drew carry a four-foot-long plastic blue barrel that was warm to the touch and seemed to weigh 120 pounds out of Drew and Stacy's bedroom and load it into Drew's SUV, after which Drew drove him home. Morphey testified that the next day, he was hospitalized following an apparent suicide attempt, having overdosed on pills washed down with alcohol. Under oath, Morphey said that Peterson had told him Stacy was cheating and something needed to be done; he had asked Tom if he loved him enough to kill for him.

A divorce attorney named Harry Smith testified that, a few days before she disappeared, Stacy Peterson had told him that she knew her husband had killed Kathleen and she was thinking of leaving him. In September 2012, Drew Peterson was found guilty of Kathleen's murder and sentenced to thirty-eight years in prison. A grand jury investigation was convened for the murder of Stacy, but the grand jury declined to indict him. She's still a missing person.

At the time of the 2012 verdict, I had begun to find my footing in my own life, but Steve lost his. Our trajectories might have been opposite, but our struggles were the same. We had both lost our fathers, and worse, the idea of who our fathers were. Too much evidence mounted: an autopsy that ruled the homicide had been staged to look like an accident, police consensus of Drew's guilt, the graphic and specific details of Morphey's testimony, along with Steve's personal witnessing of Stacy's love for all the kids, and his own experience being set up by his dad, Steve began to admit his father probably "killed two wives." When that happens, existential thoughts occur: *Now that our fathers aren't who they are, what does that make us?*

Steve and I had also been similarly accused of using our fathers' names and crimes to catapult us to some sort of warped fame—as if we weren't struggling with the idea of what our fathers had taken. When we spoke to the media, it was assumed it was to get sympathy, to make money, and/or to get book deals, all the while our main concern was how to explain such heinous acts to our innocent children—when all we both had really intended was to make the questions stop. In Steve's case, one time it was to put food on the table, once his father's pension checks were canceled.

Steve had four young, motherless children to raise. He was the only son of Drew in the home who still had a mom. I suspect that immersing himself into the formative years of his siblings' lives kept him connected to the only people who could truly understand his own confusion and loss of identity—the five of them in their father's house, trauma bonded by the pain of their paternity.

"When we moved into the house, we never thought he'd get convicted," Steve said about his father. "We thought we'd just maintain the house until he got out. I thought I'd go on with my life, and he'd go on with his, and that's that."

In fact, Steve took the master bedroom, his dad's room, where it was alleged that, if Drew had killed Stacy, that's where it happened. "It was weird at first. Every creaky noise or shadow would freak me out. We were just in a state of constant waiting, never at ease, putting life on hold waiting for the next court date."

I couldn't imagine a worse environment for Steve to move into than the house on Pheasant Chase Court, but somehow, over the course of time, Steve and his "kids" made the house their own, proving that home is where the heart is. Pictures of Stacy hung on the walls in the kids' rooms, and family photos of the six of them, including Steve's daughter, dotted the walls in the rest of the home.

THE HOUSE THAT DAD BUILT

I believe you can tell a lot about the values and dreams and personalities of a person by the house in which they live. The houses I've lived in have ranged widely—a trailer, the basement of my grandmother's house, a modular home built by a charity, the house of my ex-husband's deceased nana, an unfurnished rental, a mountain chalet under construction . . . Each dwelling a distinct slice of my life, rife with different circumstances, people, milestones, and struggles. Each part adds up to the sum of who I was meant to be.

When I close my eyes and imagine myself walking through the front door of the Habitat for Humanity house that was built for my mom, my sister and brother, and me after my father was imprisoned for life, I wince. The idea of being back in the place that holds such dark memories, scenes of my mother being brutalized by her second husband, is too much to bear. Even as a thought experiment, I reject it. I have that in common with all the families I interview—none want to go back to the scene of the crime, to the dark part of their life that adds up to their sum. In fact, it is highly unlikely for family members of perpetrators to remain in the home in which the crime took place—except in the case of Steve Peterson.

Steve eats breakfast at the table where Stacy buttered toast for her children. He showers in the place where Stacy shampooed her long brown hair. He sits in the backyard where Stacy watched her children do cannonballs in the in-ground pool. And Steve sleeps in the bedroom where Stacy's small-framed body may have been stuffed into a hollow drum and carried away. Basically, Steve tries every day to fill the void caused by his father.

All four of Stacy's children wanted to know where their mother went. They asked for their father all the time. Drew called from jail often to speak to them and made sure his monthly pension check was transferred to Steve so he could use it to support the children and pay the mortgage on the house.

"The kids asked lots of questions," Steve remembered, "and when they were little, we told them kid-friendly stories, like Dad is out helping the police find Mommy. As they got older and started to use the internet, the story became less a story and more about the truth. That's when they make you feel like an asshole for lying to them, because no matter the intention, that's what those kid-friendly stories were. School was where they heard a lot, and it would be only a quarter-truth or a half-truth of what actually happened. So, one day they were upset about feeling like I was lying to them. So I was like, 'All right, from now on, you're getting a hundred percent truth. Like it or not, I want you guys to know from me; if you hear from me, it's true.'"

There are two tragedies and two separate sets of children wondering how their grief overlapped. Stacy and Kathleen were like orbiting satellites. Kathleen's boys were grappling with the news that their father killed their mother; Stacy's children were confused, asking, "Was Dad convicted of killing our mom?" Steve would have to set the children straight on which crime was attached to whose mother. Lacy and Anthony, upon news reports of suspicious debris found in bodies of water, would ask, "Did they find our mom yet?"

Parents have difficult conversations with their children all the time, but when it comes to the talks Steve has had with his siblings, who he refers to as "my kids," *difficult* doesn't cover it. Who wants to answer questions like, "Will they ever find my mom?" or "Did Dad kill Mom?"—especially when there are no answers?

Committed to telling them the truth, Steve can only answer with "I don't know."

"I really hope they get an answer about what happened to Stacy one day," he said protectively. He has gone public with his belief that his father did kill Stacy. I suspect closure for his kids will create closure for this adult child.

Aside from grappling with his own emotions about being used and manipulated by his father, and losing his dream career because of it, as their guardian, Steve helped Drew's other children deal with their varying feelings toward their father. "Lacy went through a phase where she didn't want to talk to him and was really pissed off. Then she wanted to confront him and play tough," Steve shared. "I had to tell her not to bother; he'd just gaslight her and make her feel bad for feeling the way she did."

But that inner strength and resilience remain as Matt, Kathleen's first-born son, was named valedictorian of his high school graduation class. Steve has made sure his siblings didn't become statistics. All three boys are grown now and run a business together. They are happy and contributing members of society with a family unit that grounds them. They really lived in a place to grow.

As for Steve, at the time of this writing, his daughter is in high school and he still lives in the same house on Pheasant Chase Court with the youngest of Drew's children, Lacy, who is graduating from a nursing program and participating in a documentary about the impact of having a killer father. "I don't talk to my father really much at all," he said. "When I do, I know that everything that comes out of his mouth is a lie. But I don't regret taking the kids. If my father hadn't asked me to, I would have missed out on the biggest blessing."

CASE #5

CHRIS WATTS, FAMILY ANNIHILATOR

The trouble with what is unthinkable is that at
times it must be thought about.
—Douglas Coupland

THE CRIME

On August 13, 2018, a woman in Frederick, Colorado, grew concerned when her friend, thirty-four-year-old Shanann Watts, multi-level marketing (MLM) executive and mother of two young daughters, missed a doctor's appointment and wasn't responding to messages. Chris Watts, Shanann's husband, initially reported his wife and children missing and appeared to cooperate with law enforcement; he gave interviews to the media, pleading for his family's safe return.

As investigators looked into the case, they discovered that the thirty-eight-year-old father of two was embroiled in an affair with a coworker, Nichol Kessinger. This information raised immediate suspicions about his involvement in the disappearance of his family, as did numerous inconsistencies in his story. Watts was arrested and charged with three counts of first-degree murder and three counts of tampering with a body. The funerals for Shanann, her two daughters Bella (age four), Celeste (age three), and her unborn baby, Nico, were held in Shanann's home state of North Carolina.

While in police custody, Watts initially claimed that he had killed his wife in a fit of rage after she strangled their daughters in response to his request for a separation. Cops were skeptical, and his story would soon change. In a subsequent confession, Watts admitted not just to strangling Shanann but to smothering both his daughters with his bare hands.

The exact motive behind Chris Watts's heinous crimes remains a subject of great speculation and debate. While his initial statement to law enforcement suggested that an argument with his wife about separation and Shanann's threat that he would never see his kids again led him to snap, the investigation and his own further admissions revealed a more complex and disturbing picture. Investigators pondered the possibilities, which included:

- The extramarital affair: Watts was having an affair with a coworker, and he may have believed the only way to facilitate his new relationship was to eliminate his family.
- Financial strain: The Watts family was reportedly facing financial difficulties, including mounting debt and defaulted mortgage payments. Watts may have believed that eliminating his family would alleviate his financial burden.

- Marital issues: While the Watts family portrayed a happy image on social media, reports suggest that there were significant marital problems and tensions.

In a stunning legal development, only three months after his arrest, Watts pled guilty to the murder of his family in exchange for the death penalty being taken off the table. He was sentenced to life in prison with no possibility of parole on November 19, 2018, in a Colorado courtroom.

THE VICTIMS

Shanann Watts (née Rzucek): Thirty-four-year-old MLM professional, wife, and mother of two daughters. Shanann was fifteen weeks pregnant at the time of her murder. She had named her unborn son Nico.

Bella Marie Watts: Age four.

Celeste Cathryn Watts, called CeCe: Age three.

TODAY

In December 2018 Watts was transferred from a Colorado prison to an out-of-state facility over security concerns due to his being "a high-profile offender." One plausible theory as to what this means is that his case was well known in the state of Colorado, and so he was being threatened by other inmates because crimes against children are considered most heinous within prison walls. He is currently incarcerated at Dodge Correctional Institution in Waupun, Wisconsin. He lives in the general prison population and works in the prison infirmary.

THE MEDIA

American Murder: The Family Next Door (Netflix documentary, 2020)

Suburban Nightmare: Chris Watts (Fox Alternative Entertainment documentary, 2022)

LEFT BEHIND

Parents Cindy and Ronnie Watts and sister Jamie

CHAPTER 6

WHEN PARENTS HAVE A KILLER CHILD

LEFT BEHIND: PARENTS RONNIE AND CINDY/SISTER JAMIE

You drown not by falling into a river, but by staying submerged in it.
—Paulo Coelho

I am no stranger to graveyards. They are a regular part of my job; as a visit to the victim's headstone is on almost every call sheet for a true crime documentary. As I walked the manicured grounds on an exquisite spring afternoon in Aberdeen, North Carolina, I realized that this was my first visit to a gravesite in the South. Here, just beyond a quintessential white Baptist church complete with steeple, the birdsong sounds as sweet as pecan pie.

I had arrived at the historical Bethesda Cemetery, where Shanann Watts and her three babies now rest. A marble bench engraved with the names Shanann, Bella, Celeste, and Nico overlooks three graves. The serene setting made it hard to ponder the final moments of terror Shanann and her children endured. A truly monstrous scenario emerged in the bombshell details from a post-conviction interview conducted by detectives that became public in February 2019.

A year after Watts's conviction, investigators wearing wires drove from Colorado to where he is incarcerated in Wisconsin in a quest to, in their words, "better understand what happened when Chris Watts killed his family." The revisiting of a very much closed case only emphasized how even the most seasoned detectives struggle with the question, *Why?*

In search of some explanation, detectives set out not only to obtain more information about the murders but also to try to weed through the onslaught of false claims made by obsessed members of the public. In the lengthy recorded 2019 interview, Watts denied knowing any of the people who had popped out of the woodwork, claiming to have had romantic relationships with him. However, he offered investigators far more detail about what really happened when Shanann returned from her business trip that August night.

IN HIS OWN WORDS

According to the report generated from the interview, Chris told investigators he and his wife had sex about half an hour after she got home from her business trip at 2 AM. He told the investigators he and Shanann fell asleep after sex, but "having sex with Shanann may have been a trigger point, like you hit the push button on a bomb and it just blows up." Just a few hours later, after getting up and preparing for work, Chris woke his wife up. He said, "I felt like she knew I was having an affair. I had used my credit card when I went out to dinner with Nichol, and I couldn't ask her to pay." Chris was certain Shanann had seen the credit card charge, and the confrontation was on.

Shanann turned over to lie on her back, and Watts said he straddled her around her waist to talk. Shanann told him she knew there was "someone else" and began crying. He was concerned his wife would leave him and take the kids—that one day he would come home and she would have locked him out—so Chris denied the affair. He did tell her he didn't think their marriage was going to work. "I told her I didn't think we were compatible," he said in the report.

When he told her he didn't love her, Shanann threatened to keep the children away from him. "You're never gonna see the kids again," Watts quoted his wife saying. "You're never gonna see them again. Get off me. Don't hurt the baby." It was at that point that (according to the report) Watts strangled Shanann.

Chris said she never screamed or fought back, which remains suspicious to anyone who knew Shanann, as her personality was hardly passive. She was a fighter, to say the least. Chris theorized that noise from their struggle may have woken Bella, who walked into the master bedroom holding a blanket. She asked what was wrong with her mother. "Mommy don't feel good," he told the little girl. He wrapped Shanann's body face down in a bedsheet, which was later recovered at the Anadarko oil site where Chris worked.

As four-year-old Bella watched her father drag her mother down the stairs, she began to cry. "What's wrong with Mommy?" she asked again. He repeated that Shanann didn't feel well but told investigators, "Bella is a smart girl and knew what was going on." The sound of Shanann being dragged down the staircase woke three-year-old Celeste, he said, who was getting out of her bed when Chris returned from placing Shanann's body on the rear floorboard of his truck, which he had backed into the driveway.

He loaded Bella and Celeste onto the truck's rear bench seat, their mother's body lying at their feet. Because he did not want the girls to see their mother's face, he had placed trash bags over her head and feet; the discarded bags were later found by detectives at the site of her burial.

Chris placed a gas can in the back of the truck and got into the driver's seat. "Is Mommy okay?" Bella asked. Chris assured her that Shanann would be fine.

A neighbor's surveillance camera caught fleeting images of Watts loading his truck that morning, including the gas can he placed in the truck bed. The images do not show the children or Shanann's body. At the time the footage was released, it was believed all three females were dead when Chris drove away from the house. But the two little girls were very much alive. Bella and Celeste, each carrying a blanket and Celeste also cuddling a stuffed dog, dozed on and off on the ride to the Anadarko site, Chris said. They held each other in their sleep and lay in each other's laps, though at one point Bella told him, "Daddy, it smells." She was likely referring to her mother's body; when strangled, her bowels had evacuated.

Once at the deserted site, Chris removed Shanann's body from the truck and dragged her over to where he planned to bury her. Both girls asked what he was doing, but he said he couldn't remember what he told them. Back at the truck, Chris said, he grabbed the blue New York Yankees blanket Celeste was holding and put it over her head as her older sister sat at her side.

"He put his hand over Celeste's mouth and nose (over the blanket) and his other hand around the front of Celeste's neck," the report reads. "Bella was seated right beside Celeste as he strangled her, but Bella didn't say anything." Chris told investigators he wasn't thinking as he killed his daughter.

"If I was thinking, this wouldn't have happened," he said. "Or [had remembered] any partial hint of what I feel for those girls and what I feel for my wife, then none of this would have happened. So, I wasn't thinking."

Once Celeste was gone, he carried her lifeless body from the truck and over to one of the oil tanks, where he opened the hatch, only eight inches in diameter, and stuffed her inside, feet first, the report says. He closed the hatch and went back to the truck. Bella asked what had happened to her sister. "Is the same thing gonna happen to me as CeCe?" Bella asked her father.

Chris told the investigators he was not sure if he responded affirmatively or not. He put the Yankees blanket over Bella's head, and she cried, "Daddy, no."

Those were Bella's last words. She put up a fight for her life. He could hear her "grunt" as she tried to breathe, and her head twisted back and forth under the blanket. The autopsy on her small body showed she bit through her tongue multiple times as she struggled against her father. After using the same suffocation technique he had with Celeste, Watts carried Bella to a second oil tank on the site and stuffed her inside.

He used a shovel to dig Shanann's shallow grave and bury her, the report says. He then went to work, and on the way home, he threw his clothes and the Yankees blanket in a construction dumpster in the Watts's neighborhood.

At one point in the interview Chris mused on whether he already had the seed of murder planted in his mind before that morning. "Every time I think about it, I'm just like, *Did I know I was going to do that before I got on top of her?*

"I'd been angry since July [2018] when Shanann told me that my parents could never see their granddaughters again. I don't know if that had something to do with it, or that something inside me just triggered it, and then just all that pent up from the wedding and everything . . . it's like a long fuse that finally just went to its head."

Chris was referring to several inter-familial riffs, including one between his sister Jamie and Shanann that led to Jamie not attending her own brother's wedding.

So, that was what happened . . . according to Chris in his own words. I was present to witness the nightmare lived by the family he left behind.

> IDC [I don't care] what it sounds like. I have a soul and I adore my family. you ALL deserve to burn in Hell for supporting a bitch if [*sic*] a man who could harm his babies. You suck pigs. I hope you all die painfully. And end up in a fucking oil drum you stupid bitch. I maybe you'd prefer a shallow grave? Watching Chris's fake ass on TV pretending he didn't know where his family was was stupid as fuck. And his dumb fuck dad wanted to believe the amoeba. Chris acted like a retarded five-year-old in the police interview. And yet all he cared about was what would happen to him . . . He's a sick fucking ugly idiot from a sick fucking ugly family, You're all going to Hell. I hope.
>
> —anonymous text to Ronnie and Cindy Watts, Chris's parents

I recognize that it is a privilege for me to spend time with the Watts family, since they have not spoken intimately to anyone about all they have endured in the wake of their son's arrest and conviction. They have been barraged with hateful letters, emails, and texts like the above, for one thing. Shanann, an active social media user, frequently posted videos of family moments as well as photos and commentary. Strangers around the globe who followed the case were able to glimpse numerous interactions between Chris and his little girls, making him seem far more real to them than other family destroyers.

The Watts family members have had their boundaries invaded by this curious public, many of whom refused to leave them alone. Their silence and refusal to denigrate their son continue to fuel the internet fire, keeping an international arsenal of armchair detectives busy. They search for answers and send theories, hate mail, and requests for interviews on their YouTube channels. Some are well-meaning; most are like teenage gossips, stirring the pot; and many, like the above writer, are simply cruel.

There was so much to cover in the four days I spent with the Watts family in their home state of North Carolina, where Chris and Shanann met and married before starting a new life in Colorado. As the daughter of a murderer, I only have the child's perspective on what it feels like to be left behind. As a parent myself, I cannot imagine the pain and guilt Ronnie and Cindy Watts are enduring. I had traveled to this beautiful state to hear a mom and dad's perspective on having a child who is a killer. But first: some background tours.

At Ronnie's office, where his children Chris and Jamie ran around during their childhood, I viewed the family's history, illustrated by the photographs that line the generic white office wall row by row. Young Ronnie and Cindy with little Chris and big sister Jamie, elementary school photos, trips to Disney, Chris and Jamie in caps and gowns, then wedding finery, then with kids of their own. What I see is a beloved son who went to NASCAR races with his dad, loved the New York Yankees, and had a wife and two beautiful daughters. There is no hint of any trouble to come in these photographs.

Nor are there any warning signs in my tour of the house where Chris grew up and Ronnie and Cindy still live—though Jamie joked about the teenage tragedy of sharing a bathroom with her brother. There's a front porch made for drinking lemonade. Ronnie was raised in the house across the street; as children, the brother and sister ran back and forth between the homes so their paternal grandmother could spoil them. There are pictures and memorabilia everywhere: quilts, crayon drawings, artifacts of past Mother's Days, some from all four grandchildren. I notice some recent kind notes from strangers sending prayers. It appears to be an idyllic small-town home.

How could it have come to this? Don't ask why; don't go looking for reasons. But for Ronnie and Cindy, silencing that need to know is impossible. They are sinking in a murky water of wants. They want their grandbabies back; they want to go back in time to stop their son from doing the devil's work; they want to know what God has not yet shown them: Why?

Why didn't you just leave? Why didn't you get a divorce? Why did you also have to kill the girls? Why did you not come to us? Why did you do it?

Why won't you tell us?

Chris Watts's silence has frozen his mother and father in suspended animation—a place riddled with more questions than can ever be answered, even if their son cared to. And Chris does not care to. Says Cindy, "Over and over he tells Ronnie and me, 'Go live your lives. Go out to dinner and do things, forget about me. I'll be okay.'"

Such directives, no matter how well-meaning, are impossible to follow. The shock and disbelief are debilitating. "You're left with no real answers, or mental health answers or something, you know," his sister Jamie told me. "Because a normal guy that's never been in trouble before in his life loses his mind one night and annihilates his whole family. No, it doesn't make sense to me. None of it makes sense."

Yet here we are.

The public wonders, *How can Chris's parents continue to stand behind such a monster?* His parents have their reasons, though this married-for-decades couple, as close as can be, take very different approaches to their new reality. Cindy is simply certain "there's no way he'd kill his girls." A potent blend of biology, maternal instinct, denial, and faith makes hating Chris impossible for Cindy. If you asked her, "What's it like to have a monster in the family?" her answer would be "I don't."

"Christopher is a good person, I know him," she said. "Nobody in his past or even now, who meets him in prison, can find anything bad to say."

The family tells me they didn't get the chance to get their answers because there wasn't a trial—Chris took a plea deal in just two days—which precluded both the family and the general public from seeing the unredacted discovery (the process of obtaining evidence). This trove includes everything from text messages to crime scene photos of his children's bodies retrieved from the bottom of the oil storage tanks, a visual that even the seasoned detectives who worked the case have said they'll never forget. The approximately two hundred pages of redacted material has spared both the Rzucek and Watts families from seeing the kind of images they would never be able to unsee, and the plea deal avoided a likely sensationalized Court TV soap opera for the world's viewing pleasure. "Chris told us, I don't want to put my family through that," Cindy said.

I asked her if she thought going to trial would have helped her family release the daily unease they feel; if seeing their son go through the criminal justice system and letting due process take its course would have provided closure. "Yes," she answered without hesitation. "I would've liked to see a defense for my son, and one that would allow him to say out loud, 'I killed Shanann *but not my girls*.'" Chris's initial confession, the one in which he told police he killed Shanann because she told him she had killed the girls, is the narrative that Cindy felt "makes the most sense."

Ronnie insists there were holes and inconsistencies in his son's second confession to killing his daughters, and he spends as much time as possible in his small office tucked in the back of an auto mechanic's shop, where he has worked for more than twenty years. It is Ronnie's safe place, where he is not judged as the father who spawned a demon. I find myself feeling relieved for him; at least he has a refuge. That's hard to find for other families of high-profile murderers, as he well knows.

Ronnie sees many gray areas. His focus is not to defend his son's character, as Cindy does every moment she can; he is instead consumed with learning whether his son acted alone or had an accomplice. He also wants to get to the bottom of a question that Chris has never answered. And it's not the question you'd think. Instead of asking why Chris killed his children, he wants to know why Chris took the plea deal. Why did he avoid a trial, where the prosecution would have had to provide the full discovery? Why didn't Chris defend his character the way his own mother continues to do to this day?

Chris's father digs and digs, believing the truth is buried behind black smudge lines. He has scoured thousands of pages of unredacted discovery, obsessing over details of police sweeps of the house, cadaver dog hits, video footage, cell phone pings and records, Nichol Kessinger's Google searches. Ronnie firmly believes Kessinger played a significant role in his son's actions. If you pay any attention to the theories put forth by the amateur detectives online, there is certainly reason to believe this.

Nichol and Chris met at work; their affair had been going on for only two months at the time of the murders, yet she was already shopping for wedding dresses and googling "marrying your mistress." Data records show that she was a frequent visitor to Shanann's social media pages, where Shanann delightedly announced her pregnancy and spoke glowingly about her family. This makes it hard to believe that Nichol believed the couple had separated, as she claimed. More ominous: a truck resembling Nichol's was seen on the street outside the Watts home on the morning of the murders; records show her cell phone pinged at a tower very near the home, when she lived almost thirty miles away.

Most importantly, Chris and Nichol FaceTimed at night for almost two hours before Shanann arrived home from her business trip. Specifically, Ronnie can't let go of the redacted transcription of that 111-minute call between Chris and Kessinger, which is being withheld from the Watts family despite Ronnie's incessant pleas to review it. He believes this phone call would finally answer the question of whether his son murdered Bella and CeCe, because it is this aspect of the crime that Ronnie and Cindy cannot come to terms with.

Ronnie and Cindy did prod their son to speak the unspeakable. Holding up a paper plate during a prison visit, Ronnie allegedly waved it like a flag, begging Chris, "Will you please explain to me how you fit their bodies in a hole this size?" He didn't get an answer.

"I'm not saying he shouldn't be in jail," Cindy told me. "He killed his wife, but why the girls? There's no way he could put the girls in that eight-inch hole . . . It's not how he is, it's just not."

I hadn't wanted to pressure Ronnie or Cindy to visit the cemetery with me. I knew they had not been able to attend the funeral because of the estrangement between the two families. I realized the burial site was also a struggle for turf: who deserves to be there was the question that kept the battle raging. But on the morning I was to make the hour drive from their hometown to Bethesda, Ronnie and Cindy called to say they'd accompany me.

They brought with them a letter Chris has asked them to read at his victims' graves.

> Birthday
> 1.10.20
>
> Dear Shanann,
>
> Hey boo! Happy Birthday! Thirty-six years young today. This is the first time of year when I could always say you're "two" years older than me. You didn't like that too much, but I liked messing with you. There's so much I wish I could say to you and make up for what I did to our family. No one needed to go through this. You and our babies had a long life ahead of them and deserved to see that life. I promise the man you married isn't the man who turned his back on his family. That man was an aberration brought on by an evil outside source. You know the husband and dad I am and would testify to that today. I look outside my window and wonder what we would be doing and then I get this overwhelming feeling you're looking at me with our babies saying "We love you!" All of you are a blessing to my life and your memory lives in my soul every waking moment. I close my eyes and imagine the light of God shining across your cheeks and radiant smiles beaming down from Heaven when you look down upon us. The

love you felt down here won't compare to the love you feel up there—God's love—and I've dedicated the rest of my time on this earth to showing the love He has shown me. Cheer me on as I walk the path God is putting in front of me. I love you all to the moon and back!

Love,
Chris

The three of us walked toward the edge of the woods where Shanann and the children rest. Ronnie's phone played the song "Broken Halos" by country artist Chris Stapleton. The song is about angels who are on Earth only for a short time, in order to teach us lessons. When bad things happen, the song says, we shouldn't ask why, because we are not meant to know the answers.

By the song's chorus, Cindy was in tears. Ronnie put a protective one-armed embrace around his wife's hunched shoulders. Their decades of love for each other was their only strength against the constant attacks and judgment of the world. And the ongoing battle with Shanann's family, the Rzuceks.

For Shanann's family, there is no unsolved mystery; they know what they know: Chris was unfaithful to their daughter and murdered her and their grandchildren in cold blood. Their son-in-law is a monster. They engraved Shanann's maiden name on her tombstone, wiping away any significance Chris may have had to them or to this world.

As we prepared to leave the cemetery, I noticed a trail cam aimed directly at the headstone, almost camouflaged by the leaves of the tree it sat in. I asked Ronnie and Cindy what the camera in the trees was for.

"We've heard Frankie Junior had a camera on the gravesite to monitor strangers who videotape the gravesite for YouTube," Cindy answered, worried that the private words she has shared with her beloved grandchildren had been recorded by Shanann's brother, Frankie.

Suddenly, a gray truck sped up the narrow dusty cemetery road. And just like that, the vibe of a peaceful Sunday visit vanished; Cindy was visibly looking for an exit—should she go to her husband's arms or to the car? Her fear rubbed off on me. Who was this person now parking his truck directly behind our cars?

Cindy explained that it was Frankie, and that he'd probably called the police to escort us off the premises. I doubted it. He'd probably just come to confirm it was only the Watts family and not another YouTuber. Just in case, we left. On our way out, a police car pulled up behind us.

Hours later, as I was on the road, I got a text from Jamie—a screenshot of Frankie's Facebook post. "*. . . There's a LEGAL sign that states clearly, that This is private property, no video recording of our family's resting place, violators will be punishable by Law due to all the harassment we have received at our family's gravesite. It's not allowed, especially if your intention is to share it on social media for 'content' which is what happened. The police patrol the area all day long because of what we have had to deal with there.*"

Two families, destroyed.

In my experience, people who discover that a family member is a killer gradually come to a state of acceptance—a place where they understand the truth, however painful it is to hear. Ronnie and Cindy's emotions are so overwhelmingly painful they are failing to resume their lives—a state psychologists call "complicated grief." Even with overwhelming physical evidence and a confession, the underlying *whys* will not let Chris's family rest.

How could Chris have killed his girls when only days earlier, he was video-recorded giving them piggyback rides? Reporters, detectives, friends, and acquaintances have searched for just *one* person who could say they saw this coming, that Chris had a dark side or showed signs of being "off," but to no avail.

Cindy Watts has been reclusive since 2018, rarely working or even leaving the house. Always a mother, she spends much of her energy worrying about Chris and his well-being behind bars. *Has he found a purpose? Is he safe? Can he live the rest of his life locked away and have peace at the same time? Does he have enough money for the commissary?*

I spoke with Jamie, and she told me that Ronnie is still knee-deep in his pursuit of the "truth." "My dad wants to go to Colorado next to try to get the unredacted discovery," Jamie said. "I hate him going all the way over there to that state. I don't feel like they're going to want to help him or give him anything. My parents don't have extra money to just be flying to Colorado and staying in a hotel. My poor dad, almost close to seventy, still trying to find answers."

"There's something Cindy always goes to," Ronnie said, sitting beside his wife at the kitchen table, her cane leaning against her chair. "Is there something we did wrong?" This, of course, is the question that haunts all secondary victims.

"There's an *us* before August thirteenth and there's an *us* after," Jamie told me. "My parents are not even the same parents anymore. They're gone. They wake up every day thinking about the girls and Shanann, and they go to bed every day thinking about them."

Cindy believes it's their unwavering commitment to their son's character that keeps her and Ronnie going. "Any parent would do the same for their child," she said, her voice resolute. "They'd be exactly like us. They'd go down every rabbit hole and look at everything before letting anyone else tell them who their child is, or what his heart is really like."

CASE #6

MAGEN FIERAMUSCA, KIDNAPPER AND MURDERER

THE CRIME

On December 12, 2019, thirty-three-year-old aspiring vet tech and mother of two Heidi Broussard, accompanied by her two-week-old daughter Margot, dropped her six-year-old son off at Cowan Elementary School in Austin, Texas. She and her daughter never returned home to the apartment they shared with her fiancé, Shane Carey. The frantic father reported Heidi and their infant daughter missing; an urgent search effort ensued, quickly drawing national news coverage.

Thanks in part to the intense publicity concerning Heidi's disappearance, a week later, law enforcement officers, using surveillance and cell phone tracking, confirmed that a friend of Heidi's named Magen Fieramusca had been in her company the morning of her disappearance. Texas Rangers were dispatched to the home in Harris County, northwest of Houston and 165 miles from Austin, where Magen lived with her boyfriend Christopher Green.

A helicopter surveyed the area and noted a vehicle registered to Magen parked in the backyard of the house instead of in the driveway or a parking spot. It appeared to be placed there as a way to conceal it. When Texas Rangers saw a man leave the residence, they followed him to a local Target, where they observed him shop for baby clothes and baby formula. As he exited the store, Rangers questioned Magen's boyfriend.

Chris said he had been in a relationship with Magen since 2016, but they had broken up the previous March. Magen had become pregnant with his child, which is why the two had continued to live together even after they split. He said he had watched Magen's stomach grow, although she would not let him see her fully undressed due to their rocky relationship.

When a Ranger asked Green where Magen gave birth, he said he didn't know because "She's been really distant with me about that stuff. I don't know why." Recently, he said, he came home from a trip, and on the bed lay an infant Magen said she had delivered while he was gone. They named the baby Luna Mae. He seemed baffled about questions concerning Heidi, but after being shown a photo of Margot, he acknowledged that Luna looked exactly like the missing baby.

Rangers returned to the home to question Magen. When asked where she gave birth, she said she couldn't recall, nor could she produce any hospital or birth records. A search of Magen's electronic devices turned up several incriminating internet searches, including "Reasons for Amber Alert," "Amber Alert issued Austin," and 162 searches for "Heidi Broussard" dating back to December 12, the day Shane reported his fiancée missing.

Officers then searched the vehicle that was parked suspiciously in the backyard and made a devastating discovery. Heidi's body was in a duffel bag in the trunk. An autopsy would reveal she had been strangled with a dog leash, police said. Magen was arrested, and the baby was taken into child protection for immediate treatment and a DNA test before being returned to her father's care. In January 2020, Magen was facing charges of capital murder, tampering with a corpse, and two counts of kidnapping. If found guilty of these charges, she could have faced life in prison and/or the death penalty.

The backstory that unfolded shocked the country. Heidi and Magen were longtime friends; they met at age eleven at a Christian summer camp. Magen had confided in her friend that she, too, was expecting when Heidi announced her second pregnancy in early 2019. Magen was at the hospital when Heidi delivered Margot, as she had been with Heidi's son; family recalled how she insisted on holding the newborn, interrupting her introduction to the baby's grandfather.

In January 2023, after three years' incarceration, Magen waived her right to appeal and pled guilty to murdering her "best friend" (the kidnapping charge was dropped). She was sentenced to fifty-five years behind bars. The motive for the kidnapping and murder was listed as "maternal desire" by investigators. Authorities have been unable to confirm if Fieramusca was ever actually pregnant at the same time as her friend and victim, Heidi.

THE VICTIM(S)

Heidi Broussard: Thirty-three-year-old mother of two, engaged to Shane Carey.

Margot Carey: Two-week-old infant abducted for approximately seven days.

TODAY

Magan Fieramusca remains behind bars at the William P. Hobby Unit in Marlin, Texas. She will be eligible for parole after serving about half of her fifty-five-year sentence (including credit for three years served before the plea deal). She could conceivably be paroled when she is in her early sixties.

Baby Margot is being raised by her aunt, Shane Carey's sister, and is living a happy childhood.

THE MEDIA

The case was all over the media in Texas: Austin, Houston, Dallas.

Stolen Baby: The Murder of Heidi Broussard aired on Lifetime in 2023.

LEFT BEHIND

Brother Corban Bates; life changed forever December 2019.

CHAPTER 7

WHEN A SIBLING IS BONDED WITH A KILLER SISTER

LEFT BEHIND: BROTHER CORBAN BATES

"Nothing is easier than to denounce the evildoer;
nothing is more difficult than to understand him."
—attributed to Fyodor Dostoevsky

The falling foliage creates a crunchy carpet along the walking trails that are ubiquitous in the Pacific Northwest. My family is excited for the holiday season, beginning each day with brainstorming our Halloween costumes and ending with nightly bedtime swipes through Vrbo to book our long-anticipated Christmas ski trip.

We chose the iconic Timberline Lodge, famed as the filming location for the 1980 film *The Shining*, based on Stephen King's bestselling novel. Jack Torrance (Jack Nicholson) descends into madness, possessed by the hotel's dark secrets, and turns on his wife and son.

I didn't realize what I was doing. In planning a Christmas vacation, I was unknowingly letting my day job follow me home. Murder, obsession, hidden truths—this is my reality, not fiction. And yet here I was, walking into a hotel built on shadows and secrets, a place where menace lurks in every quiet corner. Timberline's dark corridors mirrored the unspoken tensions of Corban's family, a constellation of concealed horrors and fragile loyalties. I came for respite, but the hotel was already whispering my own story back to me.

My own children, now adults, have spent the majority of their lives overhearing the dark secrets of strangers and their haunting search for the answer to a question that possesses them: *Why?* My son and daughter have come to terms with their "grandfather" being a serial killer—an unwanted hand-me-down they had to find a place to store. Their answer to *why* revealed itself to be more pat than the whys of Chris Watts or Diane Downs—quite simple in fact—*narcissistic sociopathy.* I sometimes wonder at their struggle of being my children. But then I look at the booking confirmation for two rooms at the Timberline, and I'm reminded there is no struggle. We are skiing downhill, wind at our backs.

We made it. So many other families don't.

When a murder is committed, the families of the victim and perpetrator both endure a baptism by fire, and *both* are initiated into the club. They will forever be connected as a kind of kin, though one side is generally greeted with sympathy and the other with unrelenting scorn. Most refuse to see how both sides are joined by a crime, not divided by it.

Thirty-year-old Corban Bates's initiation happened around Christmastime. So, while I planned our family's holiday menu, Corban wrestled with his initiation into the club, a painful memory of a Christmastime visit to his beloved sister in prison. As he pressed his hand against the glass barricade between Magen and him, he thought, *Sister, have I lost you forever?*

As if she had telepathy, Magen placed her hand to meet his and said, "Brother, I swear I can feel that."

To which Corban replied, "That's because I'm sending you love."

For most of us, that exchange seems impossible to square. How can love reach across such a divide, against the weight of the unthinkable? But for those inside the circle of family, it is the most natural response. That instinct to send love, to feel it still, is not weakness; it is informed by bias. And bias is its own kind of gravity: pulling us toward the people who share our blood and history, even when the world says we should push them away.

Corban's initiation ritual was somewhat different from that of many of the other family members profiled in this book. Certainly, he suffered through the familiar stages of shock, denial, and bargaining, but the media storm never arrived. Because Corban has a different last name than his infamous sister, Magen Fieramusca, and lives far away from his family's native Texas, he has the luxury of obscurity, if he wants it. But like many family members I work with, he felt defending his sister's character was worth the risk of judgment, which is why nearly a year after his sister pled guilty, when I was preparing for my respite at the Timberline, Corban reached out to me.

> Hi there,
>
> My name is Corban. I created this account to try and get in touch with you, as I don't really use my LinkedIn account. I'll get straight to the point—I listened to all your podcasts, and I think I need you to help me tell my sister's story. Her name is Maygen Fieramusca, though it'll probably show up as Magen on a Google search. I hope you can help me, but I understand if you can't.
>
> Kind regards,
> Corban Bates

Hi, Corban,

I'm familiar with your sister's case. I'd like to talk to you.

We exchanged phone numbers, and when Corban called, I realized from his area code that he was close to where I lived, so I asked to meet him in person. As I headed to a nearby coffee shop on a brisk fall morning, I didn't yet know how I could serve Corban.

When I entered the building, Corban was already in line to order our drinks. Because we are members of the same club, I felt the urge to hug him hello, but I managed to override the instinctive impulse.

In Portland, Oregon, the sun shines as infrequently as the rain pours in California. On this day in the downtown Pearl District, some welcome sun allowed our meeting to take place outside, seated at a small bistro table. When we sat down with our drinks, squinting into the sun, I asked Corban to tell me how his journey started.

It started, of course, as it always does, with breaking news . . . this time the story of the disappearance of a young mother in Austin. That was the beginning of Corban's nightmare, though he was spared being hounded by the press, as other members of his large family in Texas were. Still, immediately, the case blew up online. As Corban was featured on Magen's main Facebook photo, countless amateur internet sleuths were going crazy trying to figure out who he might be. Corban immediately deactivated all his social media accounts and lay low. He had only one goal in mind: come to terms with this unimaginable event and try to support his sister.

Time after time, no matter the specific details of the case, there's always—often only—one big question. The media, the families of both victims and perpetrators (like my own children), the public . . . they all just want to know: *Why? Why do people do the unimaginable?* I wanted to hear Corban's perspective. Why would Magen, who Corban sweetly refers to as simply May, murder her best friend, kidnap her infant, and pass it off as her own child? "I know why," he answered. "May just wanted to be loved. She wanted a family. She had a lifelong desire to be part of a family . . . starting with the one she was born into, where she was continually abused, kicked out, left behind . . . sometimes allowed back in only to be rejected yet again . . .

"Look, I know what the world saw: an unhinged murderer who stole her best friend's baby. I want people to know that she is more than that," Corban said.

Corban bears the burden of thinking he has an answer to that age-old question of *why*. So, will it make a difference? To you, to me, to the family of the victim? To Corban? "Telling her story is all I can do with my rage," he told me. To that end, he generously shared an extensive oral history he had given to Magen's defense attorney in an effort to provide context for the murder trial that never happened. It was a chilling, tangled account of a daughter who fell through the cracks, and a family where both the parents and the system failed their many children.

FAMILY NEBULA

There is a five-year age gap between Magen and her half brother Corban, but their sibling bond is whole. The ancestral history Corban once sketched for his sister's public defender looked less like a rooted family tree and more like a hazy constellation in a shadowed sky—points scattered across darkness, some connected, some left dangling, their meaning clear, only if you knew where to draw the lines.

Magen and Corban share the same mother, Maureen, but have different fathers. Corban's father, Carl, who had one child from a previous marriage, married Maureen when Magen was about three, although Corban is unsure of their wedding date. Corban was the first child between Carl and Maureen, and nine more—including a set of twins—would follow. In all, thirteen children orbited within this family system.

Corban and Magen never called each other by their first names. Instead, it was always "Sister" and "Brother," as if naming each other anchored them against the drift of a family that was less blended than it was cosmic. Not a smooth merging, but a sky crowded with stars—some blazing bright, others faint, and still others present but invisible to the naked eye. Every constellation is like that: part seen, part hidden, part imagined. Their family, full of secrets and shifting orbits, was no different.

Trauma is a cruel unifier. According to Corban, early trauma was what bonded Magen and Corban in their religious Christian household. Thirteen children turned to an unofficial ten after Carl's eldest son from his first marriage became estranged and then Magen and Corban were, as Corban remembers it, "kicked out" of the family: Corban for being gay; Magen for refusing to remain silent about dark family secrets her parents were hellbent on keeping from getting out. According to Corban, Maureen and Carl didn't give details to the rest of their children as to why Magen and Corban left the pack.

"They just told the kids we went away from God and away from the family," said Corban. "And they needed to pray for us."

What the kids didn't know growing up is that their father is a registered sex offender.

"She was abused her whole life," Corban said, playing the role of fixer for his sister's character. I could tell it meant a lot to him to make clear the depths of Magen's void. "But I didn't find out 'til I was fourteen that my father was a registered sex offender when one of my friends gave me a printout of the registration. And then after confronting my mom, she told me the same story that they always tell everyone: that it happened one time and he was sleepwalking and woke up in bed with May and then tried to kill himself over it . . . and blah, blah blah."

By the time Corban was eleven, he was put on antacids for stomach issues and remembers the physical and emotional abuse vividly. "They would spank us with cardboard rods like the ones you find on wire hangers," he said. "They found out I was gay by hacking into my MySpace account. And after I was outed, they wouldn't let me sleep alone. They made me sleep in their bedroom until I ran away two weeks later. My dad made me stand at the end of his bed and threatened to beat me with a belt until I gave him passwords to all my social media. Essentially, they were trying to change my sexuality by making me read books. I had to sleep on a mattress in their room. They thought I was possessed by 'demons of homosexuality.' They made me quit my job. I couldn't see any of my friends."

Corban painted a picture of a little girl so frightened that she would make a wall out of her stuffed animals and hide under the bed because it would take her abuser longer to get to her.

Corban continued, "My father was the real monster. Not only am I convinced he molested Magen, I am pretty sure he did it to me. After a couple of years with no contact, I was in Texas for a wedding; it happened to be my birthday. I thought I should stop by to see the kids . . . one last try. As I was leaving, my father said something to me out of the blue. 'You don't remember, but I used to take you to the house on Waterfield and we'd wrestle.'" An innocent remark, perhaps. Corban said nothing and walked out. But those words never left him.

Magen attempted to run away at the age of eight. By the time she was in her teens and twenties, years of rejection and not being protected or heard led to resentment and insecurity. At the age of nineteen, she had a short marriage to a man named Mark Fieramusca. Before that, she left home to attend school in other cities, staying with friends. At fifteen, she moved out to go to a school that recruited Magen to play volleyball. Anything to escape Carl.

"I mainly tried to come up with ways not to be home," Magen wrote in an email to me on September 26, 2026. I had reached out to Magen as part of a documentary about the case, during which Corban provided us with a handwritten letter of Magen's alleging Carl's sexual abuse.

"It wasn't until I had moved to Portland, started therapy, and come to terms with a lot of things for myself that my older sister and I truly connected on a deeper level. I was about twenty-two years old when Magen and I met up for drinks, and for the first time deeply discussed how truly fucked up our childhoods had been. Just the two of us; we sat in a bar and talked and talked for hours. I heard a lot of terrible stuff. Like what happened when she had tracked down the family at their new home in Dallas, when we moved and didn't tell her," Corban said.

From as far back as Corban could remember, Magen had been made out to be the problem child. Growing up, both parents told the other children, to their faces, that she was evil. They pitted the siblings against her, excluded her, and didn't allow her to spend time with the rest of the family. That was simply the way life was. As they grew up together, Magen and he mostly lived in an old house in Highlands, in southeast Houston on the San Jacinto River, where their parents had attached a doublewide trailer to the house, creating one enormous dwelling for the ever-expanding family.

"On a couple of occasions when I was about four or five, Magen acted oddly around me," Corban remembered, his face tightening. "I was confused and didn't like what she was doing: she wanted to play some weird version of "house." Even as a small child, I realized something was wrong with this game, even if the concepts of what was appropriate and not appropriate were far beyond my understanding at that time. These incidents made it easier for me to keep my distance from my older sister; we were not close at all."

Around this time, Magen's first or second grade class had an enrichment-type program to raise awareness of sexual abuse. Part of the program was teaching children they could write a letter to tell someone if something bad is happening to them. "[We] wrote our moms letter over the weekend and we were supposed to leave them for our moms in the mailbox on Monday," said Magen's September 26 email to me. "I remember coming home from school and being scared and expecting something. I am not sure what, but nothing did."

In 2002, when she was about sixteen, Magen went to school in another city and lived with a friend to get away from her parents—and Carl in particular. When the family moved to Dallas, they didn't give Magen their new address nor did she know about the birth of their youngest sibling.

Still on a quest for love and acceptance, Magen continued to give herself to her family: helping with her younger brother during his chemotherapy and moving in with her grandfather to act as his "hospice nurse" while he was dying of cancer.

"She is the only person in my family who would send me anything for my birthday," Corban remembered.

This memory formed the lens through which Corban would always see his sister. Maybe that's what bias is: the lens we can't take off, even when others demand we do.

Sister and brother agreed to wait until the summer of 2018 to tell the kids their truth, at least the ones over eighteen, some already married, some enlisted in the military, who would be old enough to handle the details about why Corban and Magen were estranged, and that it was not their choice to leave the family.

FAMILY REUNION IN RUINS

Confrontation is never easy. The risk of losing more than the peace you hope to gain is immense. This was true for Corban and Magen as the summer of 2018 closed in. Magen took her meeting with her siblings seriously enough to write out her account of the alleged abuse beforehand, organizing her memories so she could read it evenly instead of reliving it. The effort and pain it took meant so much to Corban that he kept the letter all these years. "Like an autobiography, essentially," said Corban, who was present at the meeting.

The letter to her siblings was handwritten on looseleaf paper. Twelve pages long, Magen found her own words to reveal some family secrets, including the fact that Carl and Maureen had been married before and had children with other people, and that she herself was a half sister. Mostly, the letter explained why she had been estranged from them, or why, in her words, "I don't have the same relationship with Mom and Dad that you have. Do any of you know why?"

> What I have to tell you, Mom and Dad decided years ago that you could never know. I never agreed with that, and I'm sorry I waited, but until today I didn't have the strength or the right words... When I was a kid, I was sexually assaulted by an adult. He used to come into my room when I was asleep. He would wake me up, take off my clothes, and violate me ... The first memory I have of this was when I was three. I would sleep under my bed and put every stuffed animal between me and the edge, thinking my stuffed animals would protect me. The last memory I have of this was when I was fourteen. My rapist was driving me to school. He started crying and said he had to apologize to me. I already knew what he was going to apologize for. I knew because he had had this conversation countless times already.

The letter went on to detail graphic sexual abuse, as well as recounting the story of her grade school letter to Maureen, and the point at which she felt she began to be openly ostracized.

> When I was twenty, I decided to tell Mom everything. I called her and told her about all the years, all the nights, all the places. Mom said I was a DAMN liar and I needed to get mental health, and she hung up.
>
> Early the next morning she called me and said she spoke to my rapist. She said that he had admitted that everything I said was true. I had so much hope in that moment. Hope that she would finally be a loving mother to me. That I could finally get to feel the love I see her give my siblings.

She instead said it happened so long ago, we are over it, and you should be over it, too. You need mental health so you can move on.

My already broken heart shattered. I hung up. The next day was our sibling's birthday. I called the house so many times. He finally answered, and with tears in his voice, he told me he loved me and he was sorry but Mom had said that when I call, you are all supposed to hang up.

Everything changed that day. Mom always blamed me instead of treating me like the victim I was. She always treated me like the woman her husband cheated on her with. I was used to that, but now they were taking away you. The only pieces left of my heart went with each of you.

The responses from the siblings were mixed. Corban remembers one of the siblings supported them, saying, "You shouldn't have had to carry this burden alone." Another sibling was so distressed about the allegations, he ran off in tears. Magen and Corban arrived back in Houston, where Magen lived with her boyfriend Chris, absolutely wrung out from the confrontation. They were tired, empty, depressed, and just lay around for a couple days. They had failed, pretty much, in their mission. Not only had their confrontation been a dud; Magen's life was not going well in any area.

One day she was accused of stealing money from the company where she worked; Magen's boyfriend Chris and Corban picked her up from jail the day she was arrested. "Now, I didn't think she had stolen any money . . . she wouldn't have risked committing a crime for what was less than ten thousand dollars," Corban said. "Also, my sister trusted me enough to tell me the truth; had she done it, I think she would have admitted it. She had no reason to lie to me, though I will never know."

The way Corban remembered Magen's retelling was that there was a difficult, angry coworker at her place of business, and he screamed at her one day. Magen was not the sort of person to take that lying down, and after their blowup, he just wanted her gone. "From what I heard, there was a plan to get her fired," Corban explained. "That's the story from Magen's point of view, but it seemed plausible to me."

They hired an attorney and waited the case out, Corban accompanying Magen to her first two court appearances. "She was stuck in every way," said Corban. "She was in this rocky relationship with Chris, she couldn't work a new job with charges hanging over her . . . she was trapped."

The prosecution took forever to hand over certain crucial surveillance tapes as part of the evidence. When the defense finally saw these tapes, they saw no crime. There truly was no hard evidence against her; Magen's lawyer said they had absolutely nothing on her. She had gotten a raw deal. Again. All charges were dropped, but the damage had been done.

MAYBE A BABY?

A couple months after Corban left Houston and returned to Portland, Magen revealed she was pregnant. "I was not thrilled by this news," admitted Corban. "I certainly didn't think she was in the right space to start a family; her relationship with Chris was certainly not ideal. He pretty much kept trying to break up with her, and she'd just ignore it. But a baby was coming no matter what, so I told her maybe this could truly be a new beginning; that she now had an opportunity to build a new family—and finally let go of the one that had left her behind. I had no reason to disbelieve that she was actually pregnant; that never even crossed my mind."

And then, one last familial twist: Magen found her birth father online, accidentally, on 23andMe. She got in touch with a half sister on that side, who was surprised to hear from her; the father had never even been aware of Magen's existence. Unfortunately, her biological father was very ill and on his deathbed; Magen never got to meet him. Another loss, just when she might have met some real "family."

CHRISTMAS IN PRISON

"After my sister was arrested for murder, I flew down to Texas to visit her," Corban remembered. "At the time she was being held east of Austin in Del Valle Texas [there would be two more transfers before her plea deal]. My grandmother and uncle had already been there to see her, and both assured me she was doing okay; I was rudely shocked, as she was not okay. She looked twenty years older. Face swollen, eyes puffy, she looked simply terrible. We both put our hands on the glass, saying that we wished we could hug each other. I tried to keep it light. I asked her to show me her shoes, and she asked me about my new tattoo.

"I was still hoping against hope she was innocent and assured her, 'I'm going to do everything I can to get you out of here.' Magen's response was low and muffled by the glass. I couldn't hear her words. Then she said something else I couldn't make out. I kept asking her, 'What are you saying?' And then I caught the word 'deserve.' That was the moment that I knew she had really done this unthinkable act. She looked straight into my eyes, like she was trying to see if I was going to still be there. It was the most vulnerable I'd ever seen her."

'TIS THE SEASON AT THE TIMBERLINE

There wasn't much snow out my chalet window as Stephen King depicted at his Overlook Hotel, but it was enough to keep me holed up with my new puppy. Her fluffy body was X-ratedly sprawled out on the couch as I fanned out the residual smoke left from the pot roast I burned just an hour ago. When Corban called me, I had just finished seasoning it and popped it in before running for my notepad. I had wanted to ask him about Christmastime and family and whether he thought he was biased toward his sister.

"She's always been the one who's been there for me," Corban said, voice quiet, heavy with memory. "So yeah, I'm biased. I knew her before—before any of this—and I know she was not born a monster." He exhaled, slow and deliberate, as if releasing a weight only he could carry. "For a long time after she was arrested, it felt exactly like in the movie *Inside Out*, when the Sadness character is touching the happy memories and turning them blue. Every time I had a memory of Magen before this, it had the sickest feeling attached to it . . . like a slow determined annihilation of the life I knew and the life I wanted for both of us."

These days, several years into her sentence, Corban says he thinks about Magen every day, and they speak on the phone frequently. It took a long time for Corban not to wake up furious or depressed. It took a long time for one thought not to lead into a hopeless spiral of the sequence of events that led to this point. This led to this, which led to this and then this . . . and then the worst happened, and here we were.

"I can go down a very dark hole wondering at what point such an outcome could have been averted," he said. "That would start with my father being prosecuted the way he should have been. Had Magen gotten the help and support she needed, for another. Worst, for me, had I been stronger and less emotionally destroyed by our family life, would I have seen danger signs and done something? So many ifs. But here's what I know: monsters are made, not always born."

Yes, a grave injustice had been done to his sister, but even accepting Corban's account of repressed childhood memories, the comparison does not resolve or excuse the conduct at issue. Even Magen herself acknowledges that a dire past does not justify a dire present. ". . . Sharing anything about my past makes me feel like I am making an excuse for my actions and there is no excuse," Magen wrote me in an email on September 5, 2025. "... no matter what happened to me, my actions are reprehensible and I deserve to be where I am."

Still, Corban believes his sister's past is a cautionary tale. "I feel a grave injustice has been done to my sister," he told me. "When you sweep childhoods like hers (and mine) under the rug, really bad things can result. I mean, how does a convicted registered sex offender with thirteen children go along for years with CPS never coming over once to do a cursory welfare check? They didn't—not one time after our father was allowed to move back home, then or ever. We just fell through the cracks. No one was looking out for us.

"There were so many adults around us back then, and no one did a thing. People knew; they had to."

The premise of this book is to explore the question of what it's like to have a killer in the family, and in Corban's case, it is like being a donkey carrying another person's weight. Who am I to question what he believes about her or if he is wasting his time and energy supporting her? Who are we, the public, to demand that a brother, a child, a parent, a spouse erase the laughter, the quiet afternoons, the fleeting moments of joy, as if they never happened? Who are we to believe these family members are horrible for even speaking of the happier times?

This book isn't supposed to answer the question of why Magen Fieramusca did the unthinkable. It's understanding *how* Corban can still love her. To some, Corban's loyalty looks like blindness. But what if it's simply bias?

And what is bias, really? We treat it like a flaw, a distortion of judgment. Yet isn't bias also what bonds us to family, what makes us defend them, hold them closer, even when the world recoils? Maybe bias is not the enemy—it's evidence of human connection.

Science would say we're wired for it: parents instinctively protect children; siblings carry shared history like a language only they can speak. Sometimes when someone we love commits the unthinkable, even if it's not murder, we are forced into an impossible split: to accept the terrible act but still insist that the person we knew is not reducible to that act. That they are not only the worst thing they have done.

The public doesn't share that wiring. They see the crime without the context of Christmas mornings, inside jokes, whispered secrets. They conflate deed with being because they don't have the lived intimacy that blurs those lines. After meeting with Corban and having the honor of receiving his honesty, I realized that for him, bias is not denial; it's survival. It is how he continues to wake up each morning, hold on to memory and love, and make sense of the unimaginable.

CASE #7

CHRISTINE VARNESS, SLAYER GRANNY

THE CRIME

On January 2, 1991, Judy Wilkenson, Lois Huysman's neighbor, contacted a neighborhood watch in Yakima, Washington, to share her concern that she had not seen Lois in four months. Judy told detectives that she had confronted Lois's daughter Christine Varness about her mother's whereabouts. Christine lived only streets away and had full power of attorney for Lois. After Lois had hip replacement surgery, Christine had taken on a caregiver role, frequently tending to her mother's daily chores, errands, and personal hygiene.

Christine told Wilkenson, "My mother went to Seattle." When asked when Lois would return, Christine said, "I don't know." After more time passed with no sighting of Lois, Wilkenson along with other neighbors and family members questioned the story that Lois had left to travel with her new lover. Christine told inquirers that her mother had gone to Hawaii where her second home was located and would soon head to Europe and then return in August 1991 to be remarried. Christine claimed this was communicated through letters Lois was writing her, with instructions on what to do with her possessions, including returning a recently purchased Chrysler LeBaron. People who read the letters stated they "didn't sound like something Lois would say."

When police confronted Christine about the neighbors' and family's concern for Lois, Christine said, "Mom has done this before. Once she left for three and a half months with an ex-husband to Hawaii. She has also run off to Anchorage before."

It was no secret that Lois's personal life was storied, with five ex-husbands and children from many of the relationships. Despite that, friends and family insisted Lois would not slip out of her life in such a way, in particular leaving her beloved father with whom she was in constant contact and who was declining in health.

Flowers and letters were sent to concerned friends and family members, all purported to be from Lois. Letters postmarked from Redding, California, raised more red flags, as Christine's husband Doug had an ailing brother living there, and Christine and Doug made trips to visit him.

One such card with flowers supposedly sent to Christine from Lois said, "They say you lose it at 41—don't worry, you get it back at 61. Have a good one!" Persistent calls and letters from Wilkenson to the police along with calls to detectives from Lois's eldest son and daughter-in-law aroused the police's suspicion. What was first considered an innocuous case of a grown woman living her life on her own terms escalated to a missing person's case.

Investigators discovered that no passport had been issued to Lois, making international travel impossible. Social security payments continued to be directly deposited into the joint account of Christine and Lois, and Christine sold the Hawaii house and kept the $60,000 from the sale of the home, claiming she used the money to maintain her mother's main house in Yakima.

When social security payments were frozen until Lois could be proven to be alive, Christine became angry. She also became irate toward neighbors who continued to press police to question Christine's innocence.

It was close to two years since Lois had gone missing when police finally got a search warrant of Lois's home and of Christine and Doug's home, where they lived with Christine's twenty-year-old son. Lois's home was described as being maintained, but food in the home had expiration dates that were not of the current year.

Closing in on Christine as a person of interest, police presented a warrant to Christine's husband, Doug. Several items were collected, including a set of five knives, with one knife missing, a cement trowel, and a hacksaw from the garage. A card from Christine to Doug and other writing samples were collected and sent to a forensic handwriting analyst who concluded the letters written by Lois were indeed in Christine's handwriting.

Lab reports were positive for trace amounts of blood on Lois's bathroom wall and in the sink.

Finally, on July 9, 1992, Christine Varness left a letter in Doug's car telling him she had gone to the police to confess. When police questioned Doug, he was said to be shocked by what Christine said she had done.

After Christine's confession, police discovered Lois's jawless skull and an artificial hip joint encased in concrete in a Yakima storage locker.

Christine told police she had drowned her mother in a bathtub in September 1990. According to *The Seattle Times,* she said she became enraged when she tried to discuss her feelings about sexual abuse by a stepfather. Christine said her mother told her she was aware of the abuse, which allegedly occurred when Christine was between six and ten years old, but blamed Christine, rather than her then husband.

Christine's confession intimated that because Lois's lifeless body was too heavy for Christine to lift and remove from the home, she cut Lois's corpse into eight pieces, six of which were discarded at a suburban landfill. In her confession, Christine stated that for two days while her mother lay in the bathtub, she could hear her mother's voice. "I needed her to shut up," the report says. So she posthumously cut her mother's jaw out.

THE VICTIM

Lois Huysman: Age sixty-one

TODAY

Yakima County prosecutors believed the motive was for financial gain. However, Christine's defense stated she suffered from battered person's syndrome, which left Christine traumatized from sexual abuse. She pled guilty to second-degree manslaughter and was sentenced to two years in prison, with a restitution payment of $140,000.

Christine Varness is alive and a free woman, still married to Doug and living in the same house a few streets away from Lois's. She is a grandmother and a great-grandmother.

THE MEDIA

Virtually no media coverage—a total of about a dozen paragraphs in only two articles in *The Seattle Times* in 1993.

LEFT BEHIND

Kourtney Nichole, granddaughter

CHAPTER 8

WHEN GRANDMA'S HEIRLOOM IS HOMICIDE

LEFT BEHIND: GRANDDAUGHTER KOURTNEY NICHOLE

Not everything that is faced can be changed, but
nothing can be changed until it is faced.
—James Baldwin, "As Much Truth as One Can Bear"

Who else out there knows someone who killed another person?" That was the question a TikToker posted to thousands of users during the 2020 pandemic. By April, a month after the country "locked down," the then two-and-a-half-year-old social media company surpassed two billion users. One of those users was Kourtney Nichole. And she has a killer in the family.

A self-proclaimed true crime junkie, Kourtney's algorithm fed her videos by content creators who focused on high-profile crime cases and sleuthed for information as armchair detectives. A new mother living in Seattle, Kourtney had downtime and searched for ways to engage and connect during a time of widespread isolation and pandemic stress. Kourtney made a bold move. She responded to the post.

"Finally, something I can relate to," began Kourtney's inaugural post. "My grandma."

Her hair in modest braids and wearing a baby-blue cable knit sweater, Kourtney launched into a murder tale—that in 1992 her grandmother Christine had confessed to murdering her own mother, Lois, in 1990 and served two years in prison after pleading guilty to second-degree manslaughter. The time stamp of Kourtney's video was 12-30-20, only two days before the New Year would ring in, an opportune time to unburden herself of a family secret shrouded in mystery.

The video was straightforward, unemotional, detached. For the twenty-two-year-old, the nineties might as well have been the Victorian Age, ancient history, and nothing to do with her life and current loving relationship with "Grandma Chris."

Kourtney tagged her post: "#stitch with @trevercarreon TW: 'dismemberment' sort of. I've never told this story before 🤭 #truecrime #truecrimetiktoks #storytime #family #crazy." And for the first time she put on display her family heirloom of homicide in fifty-nine seconds:

> My grandma killed her mom. So, she killed my great-grandmother. It's kind of a crazy story. But back in the nineties, my grandma was over her house giving her a bath. She was elderly, so my grandma was kind of in charge of taking care of her. During the bath, my grandma brought up the past about how she was abused as a child by one of her stepdads, and her mom basically admitted to knowing about the abuse but blamed her for it, instead of the stepdad. Which sent my grandma into a rage. She ended up drowning my great-grandma. After she was dead, instead of calling the police, she cut up her body into eight

> different pieces and put them in garbage cans, filled the cans with cement, and put these garbage cans into different storage units all throughout my hometown where I grew up. When the police were investigating, she lied and said my great-grandmother was in Hawaii with this wealthy man she met. And she even faked letters from her. It's pretty crazy.

Within hours, the post metered thousands of views and currently has more than 20,000 comments.

Granny slayed

Really calling out you grandma danggg

Great grandma kinda had it coming especially knowing about the abuse

We stand with Granny

Good for her

I don't blame her

Comments led to further questions, not about Grandma Chris's "why," but about the lies and the dismemberment. The unexpected curiosity of the virtual community gave Kourtney an idea. She began a two-part series unpacking her grandmother's crime, including reading the letters her grandmother admitted to writing, pretending to be her mother, Lois, from a romantic runaway rendezvous with a lover named "John." The letters were even postmarked from Anchorage and California, hundreds of miles from Yakima, Washington, where the crime had been committed and where Kourtney grew up spending summers and weekends at her grandmother's home.

With more people viewing her videos, Kourtney began a TikTok channel, "Crime with Kourt." Four years later, Kourtney has more than 1.5 million followers who tune in to hear her commentary on famous cases, including the most recent appeal of Lyle and Erik Menendez. It was Kourtney's comparison of her grandmother's abuse story to the famous Menendez case and the alleged abuse they say they suffered that led me to contact her. A nationwide debate as to whether childhood abuse is a justifiable reason for parricide had been sparked by the December 2023 parole of Gypsy-Rose Blanchard, notorious for having her mother Dee Dee murdered by her internet boyfriend. Around the same time, the Netflix release of Ryan Murphy's interpretation of the Menendez brothers called *Monsters* had the public divided on the "abuse excuse."

Since she was two generations removed from her grandmother's crime, I wondered whether Kourtney believed abuse was a good enough reason for her grandmother to murder. But more than that, Kourtney represented what the future holds for families with killers in the family. Her grandmother's crime and conviction happened well before Kourtney's birth. It got me thinking how a family history of violence is passed through generations in storytelling (oral, written, and now the modern twist via social media) and how future generations reconcile with their ancestors' crimes. Do they worry about DNA? How do these dark family history stories get told and passed down? At what generation do we stop looking at our family history for its darker secrets and at what generation does it stop affecting us?

Kourtney is the same age as my children, who also have a killer grandparent, and who received the news of their grandfather's truth with a mix of fear, curiosity, sadness, and a compassion for me, as they learned more about my journey toward healing. While at first, the medium I chose to share my story was television and then documentaries, I related to Kourtney's TikTok fame, as I had experienced my own viral TikTok moments when sharing taunting letters my father sends me. It's both humbling and comforting when your sharing is met with an overwhelming number of views and shares. (As long as you learn to not read the cruel comments.) A dialogue happens very quickly, and you realize how many people in the world relate to you, even if they don't have a killer in the family. Often, they've been betrayed or abandoned, lied to or discarded, just like I felt, and just like other family members of perpetrators experience. The circumstances might be unique, but the emotions are universal. And so is the urge to survive it.

As I considered including Kourtney in this book, I thought back on all the cases I've been connected to and how her experience has differed when it comes to the media. The family members I work with usually have been traumatized by a relentless media disinterested in privacy or practicing compassion for families of perpetrators. But Kourtney's case is unique in that her grandmother's murder received no press. In fact, only two articles in *The Seattle Times* were published in 1993. Between the two articles, just twelve paragraphs total were dedicated to describe the crime and Christine's conviction. Kourtney, unlike other family members profiled in this book, had not run away from the public eye but solicited it behind the safety glass of social media.

"The comments mostly showed support of my grandma," Kourtney told me on a Zoom call. "That surprised me, and I wanted to share them with my grandma. I'd been afraid to tell anyone in my family, especially her, that I had decided to go public with her story. I showed my grandmother the comments, which were mostly favorable, offering her prayers and saying things like 'we hope she finds some peace.' My grandma really liked that."

It was important to Kourtney that her grandmother didn't resent her for airing the dirty laundry of the family, a practice older generations preach against but the TikTok generation seems to thrive on. "My grandma was always such a great grandmother, and what she did does not change my love for her."

Christine Varness is seventy-five years old and still lives in the house she was living in at the time of the murder. It's the same house in which Kourtney spent summers and weekends with Grandma Chris with her sister and cousins. "My grandma was always so much fun. We put on plays for her and my grandfather, did arts and crafts, like building bird houses, carved pumpkins in my grandfather's workshop, where he had so many tools from hammers to hacksaws," Kourtney said, wearing a nostalgic smile. "She had this really cool sports car that she kept in the garage and none of us kids could touch. I think it was a Firebird, and I remembered it had iridescent paint that changed colors in the sunlight. I thought it was so cool and she was so cool when she drove around town in it. I just remember my grandma always being so present in the moment when we were there. Everyone loves my grandma. Growing up, we'd go into local stores and everybody knew her. My dad is a die-hard mama's boy, too."

Christine's personable and neighborly nature is one of the reasons why Kourtney found the circumstances of the murder hard to accept. "I wish I had found out in a more sensitive way," Kourtney explained. "It was just blurted out to me in the heat of a conversation with my mother's brother, Uncle T. He just said, 'You know your grandmother killed her mother.' And I thought, 'Okay, maybe it was accidental.'"

Kourtney was just twelve years old.

"I had known that my parents had a contentious divorce, and that my mom and Grandma Chris didn't get along. And my other grandmother, my mom's mom, did not approve of my mother and father's relationship. I'm sure she didn't like Grandma Chris. In that moment of blunt truth, it suddenly all made sense as to why," said Kourtney. "But that was the end of the conversation. I was blindsided but didn't get follow-up information. I spent a whole summer at Grandma Chris's after that and didn't say a word that I knew the truth about her. The only thing I could think to do was google her. I only found two articles about her that said she cut her mother's body up, and that's when I knew it wasn't an accident and began to have nightmares."

Kourtney had never told anyone what she knew, not her father, not a best friend growing up. "It was my sister who actually confronted my grandmother for a school paper she was writing," Kourtney recalled. "I remember my grandfather getting really defensive, saying 'well, what was she supposed to do?' My father was even more protective. He always sees the best in her. The one and only time I asked him about the murder, my dad just said, 'If you did anything like this, I'd be by your side.'"

Kourtney didn't pry past the official family narrative of sexual abuse and post-traumatic stress. Grandma Chris had been triggered when her past abuse had not been validated, then victim shamed by her own mother, and that was the end of the story. Narratives protect us; they make peeling away layers feel unnecessary. The stories we stick to, especially ones told as vaguely as Christine's, help us rationalize, justify, and retain the image of the person we love. This is one of the most difficult aspects of having a killer in the family: reconciling that a person you love and trust unconditionally has suddenly been split into two, like Mr. Hyde showing up out of nowhere and moving into your house.

But for Kourtney the narrative seemed to be stalled by omissions. The people surrounding her were all active participants in Christine's life when she committed the murder and must have known more than the abuse story, but they weren't sharing. In 1993, Kourtney's father, the only biological child of Christine, was around twenty years old and still living with his mother when she was writing letters pretending to be Lois from Hawaii. He had begun dating Kourtney's mom not long after Christine got out of prison. I was curious as to whether she thought it was odd that her mom got serious with her dad even after finding out what Christine had done.

"It's easy to think about the murder as being an isolated incident. So, I guess my mom was thinking this had nothing to do with my dad," she said. "But one thing I genuinely can't understand is how my mom felt comfortable leaving her babies alone with my grandma knowing what she did, even though the incident was isolated. I don't think even a decade had passed by the time we were left with grandma. I don't think I could do that. I would wonder if anyone could be healed after going through something like that."

The older Kourtney got, the absence of the facts of her grandmother's crime began to instigate her imagination. Growing up with a killer in the family, voids can expand wider and deeper. Without explanations or discussions that aim to fill them, the imagination will step in to do it, usually conjuring theories much worse than the truth. Not talking about family secrets can hurt and make things worse. Finally, with questions rolling like credits in the movie of her mind, Kourtney requested the court files from the district attorney's office in Yakima.

"I was shocked as to how big the file was," Kourtney said, while pressing send on an email that shared some of files with me. "I learned more of the gory details that nobody wanted to talk about. I had to stop reading and put it away. I had nightmares, even though I wasn't even alive when this all happened."

Reading through the detective's report, I was eerily familiar with the street names, since the crime happened in Yakima, the same town I had grown up in with my dad, and only three years before his 1995 arrest as the notorious Happy Face Serial Killer. What also struck me were the gruesome details and Christine's reduced charge of second-degree manslaughter from first-degree murder.

The defense claimed Christine suffered from battered child syndrome (BCS), which is a diagnosis adjacent to the controversial defense known as battered person syndrome. Both are subcategories of PTSD. The BCS and the post-traumatic stress Christine was said to have exhibited when she drowned her mother became the accepted legal defense of her parricide.

Despite the fact that the allegations of Christine's childhood sexual abuse at the hands of an estranged stepfather were not substantiated, the defense worked. Character witnesses for Lois who stated she was a kind and attentive mother were ineffective. Despite the dismemberment and persistent lying about the whereabouts of Lois, which included plagiarizing letters, the judge allowed the lesser plea and sentenced Christine to an astonishing two years.

"Reading about the lies and the body parts actually made me sick," Kourtney admitted, as we discussed any suspicions she may have had about the validity of the defense and the sentence itself. "It was an isolated incident against her mom, but dismemberment is a very hard thing to do to an entire body. Why not just call the police after the drowning? Talking to my grandma and being around her, you would never think she was capable. One thing that is curious is that the judge didn't make her go to therapy or anything when she was paroled. If you let such a defense stand and she was abused so badly that she would do such a heinous act, why wouldn't you at least mandate her to get help for her trauma? Instead, she just went home like nothing happened."

But further probing of the court files revealed to Kourtney that so much more had happened.

According to Christine's July 9, 1992, confession, she drowned her mother and left her body in the bathtub for two days, while Christine returned to her own home only streets away. She couldn't move the body by herself, the weight of Lois's corpse being too heavy. What went on in her mind during those two days? Did she begin hatching an escape plan? What inspired her to consider dismemberment? What made her think to write the letters? How would she be able to keep this from her husband and son?

Still not ready to confront her grandmother, Kourtney continued to probe the confession, which explained that in order to remove Lois's body from the house, Christine used a knife and a handsaw to cut up her mother's body into eight pieces. Six pieces of her body were put in garbage bags and dumped at the local landfill. Lois's head and synthetic hip joint were each placed in a bucket that Christine filled with cement. The cement dried at Christine's house for three days and the buckets were placed in garbage cans. Christine transported the two garbage cans to a storage unit and locked them away.

How did she manage this without getting caught, without being seen, and without any additional muscle to help? How did she keep her husband from noticing the cement drying in the backyard or the missing tool from his workshop? What happened to all the blood that must have filled the bathtub? How did she scrub it so well only trace amounts of blood were found by the lab? Did she really act alone? For Kourtney, the more she uncovered, the more the single thread of the abuse narrative frayed.

"The one thing that sticks in my head when I think about my grandma is the two years of telling stories to everyone, especially police. The letters were so detailed and creative. That, and how she did what she did with the body . . . the landfill, the garbage bags, and the part about cutting out her jaw because her mother wouldn't 'shut up.'"

Will Kourtney ever ask her grandmother to share her story in her own words? Did our interview for this book inspire Kourtney to think about confiding in her grandmother or other family members? Have some of the questions I posed to Kourtney stuck with her or urged her to research more?

"I still haven't talked to my grandma about her story, actually, even after I agreed to speak to you," Kourtney said. "I do really want to, as I think it would help me understand that period of her life, but I also think it may help her heal, too. I feel like I haven't brought this up to her yet because I think it's something I need to do in person, and I live in a different state than her. That, and I have to work up the courage! I would never want to make her feel like I'm judging her, or only wanting to hear a 'juicy' story. I know that this is a serious matter, and I guess I just want to make sure she is ready to talk about it. Plus, I feel like it's more meaningful in person. I can be there for her if it starts to get hard to talk about certain things."

We discussed how adulthood and having children changes perceptions of family narratives. As we mature, we understand more about how people relate and the nature of truth and lies. I wondered if Kourtney looked at her grandfather and father differently, since they had gone through their own tragedies and loss all in secret.

"After reading the case files, I look at everything differently," Kourtney said. "The reports were detailed about police going through each room of Grandma Chris's house and gathering evidence from places I spent my childhood in. They took a Sidney Sheldon book from a rolltop desk, a desk I had admired so many times. They swept the hot tub room, an adult-only room off limits to us kids. Reading a play-by-play of the police going through each room of the house was like my own personal game of Clue."

Discovering you have a killer in the family changes the context of the content of your life.

Kourtney had found some solace in publicly discussing her grandmother's crime, but she wasn't the only one who had a killer in the family. Had she ever wondered how this affected her dad? What was it like for him to have his beloved mother in prison for two years? Did he visit his mother there? How did he grieve the loss of his Grandma Lois? Did anyone in the town treat him differently once Christine was arrested and convicted?

"I would absolutely love it if my dad and my grandpa would be involved in a conversation," she said. "I think their insight would provide new meaning to the case."

Talking with Kourtney and raising these questions, I realized I was the first person to sit and mull over the case with her. What might seem to be obvious to me was being presented to Kourtney for the first time. Our interview was the first time Kourtney stepped out from behind the court documents and began to consider other narratives that might be missing from the official one. Does she think she will process her grandmother's story differently now?

"This call is definitely creating more questions for me, particularly about my grandma's siblings and their family dynamic before and after the crime. My grandma has never really spoken about her siblings, but from reading the case files I know that they all took my great-grandma's side in the aftermath. But it does make me wonder how they feel now that my grandma has been out of prison for a while, and what life was like for them during the trial. I also didn't, until now, think about what prison life was like for my grandma. It wasn't until you asked if she had ever talked about that time in her life to me, did I realize she never had, and it's genuinely made me curious! I know it was only two years, but it's fascinating to me to know that life has to be completely different there. And I wonder if that affected her healing process. I also believe that our call helped me realize that although I'm numb to the story, it's not totally normal to grow up with this history, but even so, I'm not alone."

Kourtney is the youngest person profiled in this book and represents the legacy that is inevitable for the other families we've met. Generations will pass and young people might never know what happened to their ancestors before they were born. Some might discover the stories by accident. In that way, Kourtney's exploration is relatable to any of us who wonder where we've come from or what heirlooms might be dangling from branches of a family tree. Would discovering a secret as big as Grandma Chris's change anything? What about any secret from a relative's past that casts a shadow on their character? Does it make us question our identities? Would learning something about a loved one's most shameful moments cause us to turn off our love for them?

When a crime is reported and the public spins the details in a direction that serves their preferred narrative, it is only the crime that impacts them. For people with killers in the family, the crime is only one part of a lifelong story written by memories and moments of tenderness that have the power to pull a thread of hope through a potentially bad ending. For some family members, the crime must take a back seat to save the story. Whatever the secret is, or the history, the consequences of not going along with the family narrative could be too risky to many.

"I never really reflected how this affected my dad," Kourtney admitted. "He loved his own grandmother Lois so much. He says she was so kind, which is why it's hard to one hundred percent understand how my grandma could kill her and to believe that she was so callous and cruel about the abuse Grandma Chris tried to talk to her about. I read that my dad was going around town asking if people had seen his grandma, searching for her. I felt sad for him that for two years he was being lied to by the closest person to him. But even when the truth came out, he defended his mom. To this day, he hasn't read the court files. He only knows what Grandma Chris has told him.

"Deep down I want to say my grandmother's motive was the abuse," Kourtney continued. "The money she took was not life-changing. The whole family story is about abuse, but having it being monetary would be inconvenient. These stories are happening or not happening around the world."

Thanks to a medium doubling as an online community, we see that Kourtney's story is not as rare as we think. With her willingness to release stigma, Kourtney took on the responsibility of becoming an unlikely historian of hardship.

"I might still not have known anything about this if it wasn't for my uncle T randomly saying it," Kourtney said, as we wrapped up our two-hour call.

"Are you oddly grateful to Uncle T, even if he spoke out of turn?" I asked. "Or do you think ignorance is bliss?"

"If I'm ignorant to the crime, I'd also be missing out on the story of how Grandma Chris rebuilt her life," Kourtney said. "And that is the heirloom I want to pass to my children when the day comes that I tell them about this. And who knows, if my grandmother had grown up feeling she could tell someone what was happening with her stepfather, her life probably wouldn't have come to this. In a big way, her secrets and shame are a cautionary tale."

CASE #8

THE MURDER OF NICOLE BROWN SIMPSON, CRIME OF THE CENTURY

THE CRIME

In the early morning hours of June 12, 1994, the discovery of the bodies of two young, fit, and highly attractive people in the upscale enclave of Brentwood in Los Angeles would quickly lead to an international media frenzy. Nicole Brown Simpson and her friend Ron Goldman were stabbed to death on the doorstep to her quiet condo while her two young children slept inside. The killings were viciously brutal—Nicole had been nearly decapitated, while Ron had put up a valiant fight before being overcome by numerous stab wounds. Who could have committed such a heinous crime in this sunny slice of paradise?

Attention quickly turned to Nicole's ex-husband, the genial former USC and pro football star turned popular actor, pitchman, and all-around celebrity. Nicole had married O.J. Simpson in 1985 after a long courtship, and their eight-year-long marriage was known to be tumultuous; only months before the murders, photographs of a bruised Nicole had been featured on the cover of the *National Enquirer*. But O.J. had been in Chicago on the night of June 12, flying there after his daughter's dance recital, which both parents attended . . . separately. The police called him in his hotel room to inform him of the murder of his former spouse. Professing shock and grief, Simpson immediately flew back to LA . . . and the madness began.

Nicole's funeral, where police held back the crowds and shut down the streets as the grieving family was besieged by paparazzi; O.J. in attendance with a mysterious bandage on his hand. News helicopters flying night and day over the Brown family home, seeking photos of the bewildered Sydney and Justin Simpson. And then, the event that riveted the nation . . . a slow-speed two-hour Bronco chase across Southern California the day O.J. was ordered to surrender after murder charges were filed. Ninety-five million Americans watched the slow-speed pursuit as onlookers waved signs and cheered him on, until he peacefully surrendered.

Next came the trial of the century. In a Los Angeles deeply unsettled after the Rodney King riots, Simpson's legal "dream team" zealously defended their client in front of a hapless Judge Lance Ito and an outmatched prosecution team headed by Marcia Clark. The drama was high: the glove that didn't fit, "so you must acquit." The excruciating testimony by Mark Fuhrman, whose credibility was shot by racist recordings played in court. And the endless ongoing character assassination of Nicole, a victim who had been friends with these lawyers for years and lavishly entertained them like family at every holiday. The Brown and Goldman families sat grimly through it all; Denise Brown took the stand to talk about domestic violence.

And finally, jury deliberations began in October 1995. On October 3, approximately *150 million viewers dropped everything* to tune in to see the verdict live from the downtown LA courtroom. NOT GUILTY. O.J. vowed to devote his time to tracking down the real killers.

THE VICTIMS

Nicole Brown Simpson: Thirty-five-year-old devoted mother and beloved sister, aunt, daughter, and friend

Ron Goldman: Twenty-six-year-old son and brother; aspiring actor/server at trendy Mezzaluna restaurant

TODAY

A civil jury found Simpson liable for the deaths of Nicole and Ron in 1997; he was ordered to pay $33.5 million to the victims' families: the Goldmans and Nicole and O.J.'s two children. The intention was to establish a trust for the children, but because O.J. had few accessible assets (and later faced ongoing garnishments and asset seizures), most of that judgment has remained unpaid. After winning custody of his children from Nicole's parents, Simpson raised Sydney and Justin in Florida. In 2007, O.J., accompanied by a group of friends, broke into a hotel room at gunpoint to retrieve some sports memorabilia he claimed was his; he was sentenced to thirty-three years in prison for armed robbery, kidnapping, and assault. He served nine years and was released early for good behavior in 2017. Simpson died of prostate cancer in April 2024, just weeks before the thirtieth anniversary of Nicole's death.

THE MEDIA

From the day of Nicole Brown Simpson's murder, this case captivated the world like no other and marked a turning point in "true crime." Wall-to-wall newspaper, magazine, and television coverage turned a horrific double murder case into a national soap opera replete with sex, drugs, scandal, celebrity, and money . . . and people couldn't get enough. Virtually every aspect of the media world exploded.

Magazines: Nicole Brown appeared on the cover of every tabloid supermarket magazine for six straight weeks in the summer of 1994. Thousands of features were printed about her, in every outlet from mainstream news organizations like *The New York Times* to *People* magazine to *The Globe*.

Books: More than a hundred books appeared in the second half of the 1990s, from Simpson himself, his lawyers, friends, hangers-on, and "friends" of Nicole.

Television: The countless TV movies and specials on the crime of the century started with *The O.J. Simpson Story* (1995), a quickie TV movie about the relationship between Nicole and O.J. that started shooting in 1994; it was released during his trial.

O.J.: Made in America (2016). Documentary examining the life of Simpson through the lens of race and celebrity.

Inside Look: The People v. O.J. Simpson: An American Crime Story (2016*)*. Miniseries starring Sarah Paulson as Marcia Clark and Courtney B. Vance as Johnnie Cochran.

The Murder of Nicole Brown Simpson (2019). Starring Mena Suvari as Nicole, improbably suggesting that she had been murdered by serial killer Glen Edward Rogers.

O.J. & Nicole: An American Tragedy (2020). TV special narrated by Nicole's sister Tanya.

LEFT BEHIND

Denise Brown, Nicole's older sister and lifelong best friend; sister-in-law of O.J. Simpson—life changed forever in June 1994.

CHAPTER 9

WHEN A KILLER MARRIES INTO THE FAMILY

LEFT BEHIND: SISTER DENISE BROWN

He destroyed my family. How could one person fuck up so many lives?
—Denise Brown, in *The Life and Murder of Nicole Brown Simpson*

In 1994, I was fifteen years old and sleeping on a cot in the basement of my grandmother's small home in Spokane. The bombshell arrest of my father, Keith Jesperson, was still a year away, but I was already living in a different kind of hell . . . one that is far more commonplace than having a killer in the family. The hell of living with an abuser in the family.

As I mentioned, quarters in the basement were tight. My mother and stepfather slept only yards away behind a fake wood panel, with my new half brother Jonathan in a crib sharing their "room." My stepfather had entered our lives when I was eleven years old. He was a violent and angry man who nearly killed my mother several times. A serial abuser, he put my mom in the hospital more than once and had the criminal convictions for domestic violence to prove it. To say that baby Jonathan had been a surprise addition to the family would be an understatement.

At that time, our family was on a waiting list for housing from Habitat for Humanity. A representative came to the house for an in-person meeting and assessment of our needs. My mother, stepfather, brother, sister, and I all sat in the living room upstairs for our formal interview. I was not feeling really confident about the outcome . . . I was pretty sure we wouldn't qualify. And then, out of the blue, while speaking about her children, Mom said, "And we're expecting another one."

We three kids all just looked at her in shock. The thought in all our minds was *Mom, you can barely take care of us . . . why would you have another baby? And with him?* We could not believe our ears. At the time and to this day I cannot fathom how she had allowed this to happen. I never asked her, but I can only surmise that this was just another part of her general pattern of lack of self-care, lack of personal agency, and being generally beaten down, in every sense of the word. Jonathan was a sweet baby, and we were happy to have him, but . . .

Which is why in June of that year, when the murder of Nicole Brown Simpson exploded across the country, I took a very personal interest in the case. The lurid details that were splashed across every tabloid about the abuse Nicole had suffered riveted me. Her situation was as far removed from my mother's as it was possible to be. Nicole was gorgeous, athletic, rich, confident, with a loving family. She had enjoyed a privileged upbringing; her parents lived in a gated community on the beach. She had traveled the world and was friends with celebrities and power brokers. She had married a star athlete-turned-actor and lived a dream life in Los Angeles that I could only imagine in my wildest dreams. How could this have happened to her of all people?

I met Nicole's sister Denise Brown about fifteen years later, when my first book, *Shattered Silence,* was released. Telling my own personal story certainly involved some discussion of domestic violence—the cause that Denise had devoted her life to after her sister's murder. She was tirelessly traveling the world, visiting shelters, speaking out everywhere on the topic. She also ran a small speaker's bureau for the many experts she came across in this field. The two of us met and truly connected; we talked about conferences at which I might speak. No bookings for me came of our meeting, but I had made a true friend.

Denise was beautiful, outspoken, and passionate about educating anyone and everyone about the dangers of domestic violence . . . the "dirty little secret," she called it. Denise looked strikingly like her sister Nicole; they were less than two years apart in age and had been closer than close all their lives. Denise and I shared a certain bone-deep understanding of the terrors of living with an abuser. We stayed in touch.

Jump ahead another few years . . . while in my work as a correspondent for *Crime Watch Daily*, I started thinking about the Simpson kids. Denise kindly put me in touch with Sydney and Justin, though I never worked with them; they shunned publicity and lived quiet, anonymous lives in Florida—a desire I understood very well. However, it occurred to me yet again at that time that Nicole's true story had never been told. She was always an accessory: to a football player, to the many friends who exploited their relationship with her, even at her own murder trial. Her story had gotten lost; and that haunted me. What an injustice: the trial of the century and no one knew what Nicole's voice sounded like.

In 2023 I got my opportunity: I was working on putting together one of the biggest projects of my life, a documentary for Lifetime called *The Life and Murder of Nicole Brown Simpson*. Her family members were leery; they had seen Nicole's name and image exploited for ratings for nearly three decades by this time. As the thirtieth anniversary of Nicole's murder approached, both Brown parents had passed away. Still, the three sisters, Denise, Dominique, and Tanya, were for the first time united and entirely on board with this project. They were burning to tell the story of the sister they had known and loved, to show the world the complex and extraordinary woman Nicole had truly been. The docuseries was meant to be about Nicole—her life, her legacy, her irreplaceable contributions—not about her murderer, the man whose name the world knows but Denise refuses to utter. To her, speaking it would grant him credibility and attention he never earned and certainly doesn't deserve, not even in his death. Names are for the living, for the human. Denise has never seen him as either. He was her sister's abuser and killer, nothing more. That's why his name is not included in the title of this chapter.

True crime, especially in the last decade, had become a business where people are out to make big money. This is hardly a secret; in fact, the phenomenon had started with Nicole and the circus that blew up around her murder. I was hardly on the "inside" of anything in 1994; I was a teenager living in the basement and devouring the *National Enquirer* on the supermarket checkout racks like everybody else in Washington state. Three decades later, as a busy and successful executive producer, I was constantly having to remind myself where my true loyalties lay. It is a daily reality of my working life that the worst tragedy of someone's life can mean a big payday for a number of companies and people out there. I had always appreciated the power of the media and how it can tell true stories and personal points of view, shining a light on uncomfortable truths. My goal in my work had always been to give family members an equitable share in any profits and as much voice as they could possibly have once they enter the machine. Of all the many projects I've worked on, the responsibility was terrifying.

I understood what it was like, in my own small way, to see the story told over and over by other people with their own agendas. Victimization occurs yet again when you have no control over the narrative and people are profiting off your pain: it is their entertainment and your agony. What I appreciated but certainly never experienced to the degree that Denise had was seeing the victim being completely misrepresented onscreen. My mom's personal privacy and dignity were invaded many times, but Nicole's entire life had been hijacked over and over in a large-scale character assassination in front of the entire world. Denise and her family had only rarely had a say in how their sister and daughter was portrayed. This time, I was determined to make that happen.

I was thrilled to see Denise in person again in the production company studios, but I knew what a toll it would take on her to relive the most painful time of her life, even thirty years later. Our many discussions, and several of her official sessions on camera, were frequently interrupted by tears. She became quite animated when we talked about the media frenzy that had surrounded the Brown family in the wake of her sister's murder. There was still plenty of anger and disbelief about all that had happened to them that summer of 1994.

"That 6 AM phone call from LAPD telling us that Nicole was dead was the end. The end of our family as we knew it. The end to the happy, carefree life I had enjoyed for thirty-five wonderful years. Most importantly, it was the end to my intact family that I cherished above all else. I had to come to terms with the reality that we had welcomed a killer into our family, and that knowledge is hard to bear," she told me in one of our long chats.

"That man had been in my family for nearly twenty years. The two of us were oil and water from the first time I met him, as Nicole's new boyfriend at a football game in New York. I was immediately disturbed at how volatile their relationship appeared to be. I just didn't like what I was seeing with this new guy, despite his charm offensive. But my sister's mind was made up. She was in love, this relationship was what she wanted, and she went after it. From that day on, he was in. On Christmas at my parents' house in Monarch Bay a couple of months later and every holiday from that point on. Even after they divorced! He was always around . . . and talking with my mother on the phone all the time when he wasn't actually present.

"Always there, always loud, the center of attention . . . and eventually came the wedding and new start to their relationship Nicole had wanted so much. And shortly after . . . two beautiful children. I loved Sydney and Justin with all my heart. Along with my son and Dominique's son and our brother Rolf's kids they were such a happy group of cousins. Baby showers, athletic events, vacations playing on the beach . . . it all looked so idyllic. And many of these times were wonderful, much as it pains me to say it now. We were such a happy family. We welcomed everybody with open arms. We welcomed him. We just didn't know . . ." Her voice trailed off.

THE MEDIA DESCENDS

"We were all in shock that week," Denise said. "This was the most sudden, violent, tragic murder . . . and the media was all over us while we were only trying to come to terms with this loss. I cannot begin to describe the madness that descended on our house. Nicole was murdered on a Monday; Sydney and Justin arrived at my parents' house that afternoon. My dad went to Los Angeles with my brother Rolf and sister Dominique to clear out her condo on Tuesday, while my mother and I were at the cemetery to pick out a headstone. The media was camped out there on Bundy Drive when Dad and Dominique arrived . . . stalked even as my brother washed away the blood on the walkway.

"Nicole's funeral was held two days later. Just driving from our family home to Laguna Niguel up to Los Angeles was fraught. We were being pursued by all kinds of paparazzi from the moment we left our neighborhood. They weren't hard to spot: a bunch of guys in beater cars with enormous black cameras sticking out their windows, literally chasing our procession up the freeway.

"*Someone has to talk to him. We've got to get some information out of him* . . . was what we had all decided, given that their father would be riding with Sydney and Justin. There had been plenty of discussion about who would go along with them in that particular car. Accompanying the kids was the job I wanted that day, but I was not permitted to be the one. My rage was incandescent. I could not have controlled myself in his presence.

"So my sister Tanya rode in a separate limo with the kids and their father. Later, she told us that all she could do was look at his finger the entire time she was seated in the car with him. He had a large bandaged cut on his right hand, and she could not tear her eyes away. *You killed my sister,* was all she could think the entire ride. She got no information out of him, by the way. I didn't care what he said or didn't say—I knew who had killed Nicole.

"Meanwhile I was with my parents, Dominique, and a friend in a different limo. Our driver took up two lanes the whole way: he drove right up the line between the fast lane and the next lane over on the left for twenty or thirty miles to try to shake these guys. He couldn't. It was dangerous. They were relentless. They were always there. They would be a fact of life for months to come.

"As we pulled into West LA, city traffic officers were posted to block off traffic and control access from Sunset Boulevard. We were given our own police escort. I could not believe my eyes at the number of spectators hanging on the fence outside the church; they were everywhere. People were not allowed into the actual church unless they had been invited; attendees were checked off on a list as they entered. Anyone who hadn't shown up early didn't get in at all, invited or not. It was that crowded. God knows who had been important to Nicole that we forgot or left off. We weren't really thinking clearly. It was madness. Compounded by shock.

"Going to the cemetery for the burial was another challenge. The media followed us away from the church all the way back down to

Ascension Cemetery in Lake Forest, down in Orange County. At least here they had to wait outside. However, the paparazzi had paid small fortunes to nearby residents to rent homes that overlooked the cemetery, some with perfect views of Nicole's grave. And there they all were, inside those homes, all set up with huge cameras pointing at us. Snapping away as my sister was lowered into the ground.

"Can you imagine?" she asked me. I couldn't.

Nicole had become the biggest story in the world . . . leading to one of the defining media moments in twentieth-century America. Every single person we interviewed for the documentary could clearly recall exactly where they had been the night of June 17, 1994, when the nation came to a near-halt to watch a slow-speed car chase on Southern California freeways.

In a country of 260 million or so people, more than 95 million households tuned in to watch Al Cowlings drive slowly south as helicopters flew overhead. In the backseat was his despondent best friend, who had failed to turn himself in to the police that morning. Onlookers lined the 405 and five freeways to cheer the white Bronco on, many waving signs. Friends and former teammates called in to the local Los Angeles news radio station, pleading with Simpson in real time to turn himself in. Every single network television station covered the chase live, even breaking into Game 5 of the NBA Finals. In the midst of all this, two sisters joined the madness.

"There was no time to rest, absorb the enormity of our loss," Denise recalled. "I went with the rest of my family the day after her funeral, a Friday, to finish packing up Nicole's condo . . . there were even more media and spectators camped out this time, if that's possible. I ignored them and went inside to continue boxing up my sister's life. Room by room, we dismantled the beautiful forever home she'd moved into only six months earlier. I was numb with shock on this beautiful summer day.

"All of a sudden, we heard the rotors of helicopters directly overhead. I felt like we were in the movie *Apocalypse Now* . . . under attack. I ran up and down the stairs, slamming every window and door shut. The deafening noise was echoing through the entire house. What could be going on?

"A neighborhood running buddy was one of the people outside. She and Nicole had been close, as Sydney was great friends with her daughter. I could not believe my eyes when I looked outside and saw this woman literally rolling around in the grass and wailing. Then she popped up, ran to the front door, and started banging. Drama for the cameras.

"I threw open the door: 'Leave. Now. Don't you dare even show your face here.' I didn't wait for a response, just slammed the front door shut and went back inside. I turned on a television to see what the hell was causing such an uproar. And there it was. 'Oh my god, Simpson's in a Bronco on the 405 with a gun to his head, he's on his way to be with Nicole, he's going to kill himself . . .' was the chatter on the television . . . every single station.

"Dominique and I exchanged one shocked glance and, without a word, bolted outside and rushed into her car. We both had only one thought in mind: stop him. We were not about to let that man end his life at our sister's final resting place if we could help it. Our adrenaline was soaring, and we certainly weren't thinking straight. The chase was on.

"We listened to KNX live radio as we drove. The news and speculation were nonstop. Rumors were flying: he had a mask, he had ten thousand dollars cash, he was making a break for it. That man was never headed to my sister's grave. I was told many years later that a friend of his with a boat was meeting him to help him escape out of Mexico, and to this day I believe it.

"My sister and I eventually decided to pull off the freeway. We found the nearest pay phone and dialed 911. 'This is Denise Brown calling, I'm with Dominique, we are Nicole's sisters, and we want to stop him . . . is there anything we can do?' Seriously, we were delusional. . . like we could possibly do anything about this insane media circus we found ourselves living in. The operator was courteous but brisk; the call was brief. I am sure she had some doubt that we were really who we claimed to be; and what could we realistically have 'done' anyway?

"When I hung up all my burst of energy was gone. One thing Dominique and I knew after years of him being part of our family: there was never any danger of him dying by his own hand. He was far too enamored with himself to ever commit suicide. Deflated, we got back into the car and took back roads home to Laguna while he eventually made it back to Rockingham Drive and surrendered. A week later, he was arraigned."

Denise paused. "You know, I was insane for quite some time. It's not in my nature to fall apart, but if ever there was a time I would, it was that year. Whatever I might have done, I would have copped an insanity plea. Because I was completely out of my mind with rage."

It was fascinating to hear all of Denise's inside stories about the crime of the century . . . especially the plague of the media. Her story about Nicole's friend brought up what could have been another painful memory—that of the many friends who were quick to sell Nicole out when she was no longer here to defend herself. As executive producer of the documentary we were working on, I knew I was walking a fine line. I was committed to sharing the sisters' vision of showing Nicole as she truly was. Giving her a voice. However, in the interest of full coverage, a number of friends were also interviewed as part of this program.

"Just days after my sister's murder, and all these people were saying the most outrageous things," Denise remembered. "God, did people come out of the woodwork with their stories. Each new story, worse than the last, of all that had happened to Nicole. From her friends. Who never said anything. So many people claimed that Nicole had said to them some version of 'Yeah, he's going to kill me and get away with it.' Where were they during the trial? Where were they during her marriage?" Denise asked passionately.

Some of them saved it for their book. One of the most controversial books of the 1990s was written by Nicole's friend Faye Resnick, assisted by a ghostwriter who had a day job as the *National Enquirer*'s gossip columnist. Together they produced a salacious tell-all about her friendship with Nicole. When Faye was interviewed as part of the documentary, she said, "I was told that I had credibility issues because I was in treatment and would never be allowed to testify. I was gonna get that information out there somehow, some way. I didn't care." Her efforts resulted in a number one *New York Times* bestseller . . . and plenty of backlash. Faye was heckled at many of her book signings while she insisted her real message was to break the cycle of violence.

Many others accused her of writing the book out of greed. "They said about me that I was selling her soul for money, which was so disgusting. That hurt me so much . . . I dove into the void, and I would do it again . . . the only thing I would change is, obviously, not having to go into treatment so I could have told my story on the stand and could have helped her more than I was able to."

"The controversy was that she talked about some experiences with Nicole that I would have preferred if they weren't out in the open; I would have preferred they were not in the book . . ." mutual friend Robin Greer said diplomatically on camera. "Faye felt that she also had to show some of the flaws in Nicole, and make her human. It wasn't as if she or any of us were saints."

"Yeah, all those books," Denise said, shaking her head. Faye Resnick was not the only person profiting by writing a book about Nicole. Everyone involved with this case in any way, it seemed, had a book deal. That included her killer, who was quick to get his side of the story out. In 1995, as he awaited trial for murder, Little, Brown released the book *I Want to Tell You: My Response to Your Letters, Your Messages, Your Questions*, in which Simpson protested his innocence and responded to fans offering support.

There would be more than a hundred books published about the case from virtually every major New York publisher. There were memoirs from attorneys: Christopher Darden's *In Contempt*, followed by lead prosecutor Marcia Clark's number one bestseller *Without a Doubt*. On the defense side, Johnnie Cochran weighed in with his memoir *Journey to Justice*; former friends turned mortal enemies on the Dream Team, F. Lee Bailey and Robert Shapiro released *The Truth About the O.J. Simpson Trial: By the Architect of the Defense* and *The Search for Justice: A Defense Attorney's Brief on the O.J. Simpson Case*, respectively.

Police detectives who headed the investigation told their stories: *Evidence Dismissed* by Tom Lange and Philip Vannatter and *Murder in Brentwood* by Mark Fuhrman, most prominently. Jurors from the criminal trial told their stories in quickie books immediately after the verdict in the criminal trial (*Madam Foreman: A Rush to Judgment?* by Armanda Cooley, and *The Private Diary of an O.J. Juror* by Michael Knox). Simpson's former sports agent/business advisor Mike Gilbert had a change of heart and wrote *How I Helped O.J. Get Away with Murder.*

There were definitely two camps and two competing narratives battling in the court of public opinion. Of course, Denise was offered her own book deal. "I signed a big book deal with Judith Regan at Harper Collins during the trial," she recalled. "Because I wanted so badly to tell the real story about who my sister was . . . that fell apart, fast," she said flatly. "'Creative differences,' you could say. They wanted a tabloid, sensational book, rehashing every story on the front of every trashy magazine, and I wasn't going to do it. There was not enough money in the world for me to sell out my sister in that way."

More than a decade later, trials over, while he was living a quiet life in Florida, it was Simpson's turn to sign a lucrative deal at ReganBooks. *If I Did It*, ghostwritten by screenwriter and Brentwood resident Pablo Fenjves, told O.J.'s tale of his relationship with Nicole and offered a "hypothetical" version of the events of June 12, 1994, at Bundy Drive—how it would have gone down *if* he had done it. He swore he did not.

The book was to be accompanied by a broadcast special of Simpson being interviewed by Judith Regan on Fox in late 2006. Due to overwhelming public backlash, and loud criticism from both the Brown and Goldman families, both projects were soon canceled, hundreds of thousands of books were pulped, and the wildly successful ReganBooks imprint (home of Howard Stern's *Miss America* and Jenna Jameson's *Make Love Like a Porn Star*), which had just moved offices from New York to Los Angeles, was closed down.

"Some months after this all went down I happened to run into Judith Regan at a function," Denise told me. 'You people cost me my job!' Judith said to me. 'Deservedly so,' I told her."

However, the book saga wasn't quite over. A bankruptcy judge in Florida awarded the rights to the book to the Goldman family to satisfy some of the civil judgment. The book, heavily annotated by the Goldmans, included an afterword by novelist Dominick Dunne, who had chronicled the criminal trial for *Vanity Fair* and had lost his own daughter to a violent boyfriend.

The reworked version of the book was released in 2007 by Beaufort Books. The cover art featured the word "If" in *If I Did It* in tiny type, so the new title appeared to be: *I Did It: Confessions of the Killer*. Fred and Kim Goldman made an appearance on *Oprah* to discuss their new venture; Simpson was arrested in Las Vegas on the day of its release, and the book reached as high as #2 on *The New York Times* bestseller list in its six-week stay in 2007 (the publisher claiming sales in excess of 100,000 copies).

Denise Brown decried the Goldmans' involvement in this project, given the highly unflattering portrait of her sister by her killer in its pages. "If it were Ron the one hundred pages was trashing, Goldman would never have published it. So I think that says it all," she told the *Los Angeles Times* in 2007.

"Blood money," she told me while shooting the show. "Everyone had their hands out. Everyone wanted to profit . . . but my focus had sharpened over the years. I was now heavily involved in the fight against domestic violence. Now *that* was the story I wanted to tell. Of course, no one wanted to hear much about that. I was all about supporting the work of the Nicole Brown Foundation. And there were some members of the press who helped me in that.

"Diane Sawyer was the one journalist who never stabbed any of us in the back. She was and is a class act. Geraldo Rivera had a daytime show at the time; he did a big fundraiser for the Foundation on his show, which was great. I made a number of appearances with him for a while—he was a great guy. Team Nicole all the way.

"The night the Foundation opened we did a press conference at the Rainbow Room in New York. A guy from the *Howard Stern Show* was there . . . Stuttering John, known for asking the most inane, offensive questions at press conferences. He kept shouting out questions about O.J.

"I said, 'This isn't about him, we are here to talk about the Foundation and why we founded it in memory of Nicole.' A couple more reporters asked questions, then he popped back up. 'Did you not hear me the first time?' I said. 'We are here to talk about the Nicole Brown Simpson Foundation.' He was not deterred, he shouted out again—and I had had it. I ripped off my mic and said, 'You're an asshole. We're leaving.' There was an immediate stir; a staffer approached me and tried to keep me there. I didn't slow down . . . the Browns left. The other press members there were stunned. It was a great early lesson to me on how some of them operate when you are trying your hardest to get across an important message.

"There was plenty of backlash about this. Even his boss Howard Stern was angry; and he certainly knew how Stuttering John operated. 'What the fuck is wrong with you?' he asked him on the air. 'We wanted to get her on the show and you screwed it up! What the fuck is wrong with you?'

"What was wrong with a lot of these so-called journalists was my question," Denise said.

So . . . that was my challenge. To tell the story of Nicole her family wanted told, to not be one more journalist who let them down. The sisters had opened up their hearts to me, sharing personal photographs and home movies of Nicole throughout her life, which added so much to the show. As we watched the rough cut of the documentary, I was very nervous.

"I loved it," Denise said. "You did a great job, Melissa. I can understand why some of those topics and people were included . . . but Nicole truly came across. And I learned many things I had never known before. Things that will help me going forward. Thank you," she said sincerely.

The Life & Murder of Nicole Brown Simpson premiered in June 2024 on Lifetime; a record 5.2 million viewers tuned in. The high ratings were gratifying, of course, but far more important to me was the fact that a story that had haunted me for decades had finally come to fruition, and I had mastered the tricky balancing act I must navigate for all those affected by a killer in the family. I had not let down a friend who trusted me. And, at the glamorous premiere party in Los Angeles, I thought of my mother . . . this was the kind of gathering she would never have imagined attending. I was there for *her*. I could not ask for more.

AFTERWORD

THE PHOTOGRAPH

While I must have seen the photograph before—it had survived for decades, after all—I had never examined it too closely. It suddenly became much more valuable, after I whispered to my mom, "I love you so much," for the last time.

My mother died quickly . . . so quickly, I didn't get to know the names of the angelic hospice care nurses who were ushered in and out over a short weekend. I had long ago dealt with the death of the idea of ever having a father figure. Both of my mother's "partners" had been letdowns, actual epic failures, rendering fatherhood a figment of my imagination. But, now, I wasn't just fatherless; I was motherless. Yet as I stared at the photograph, I could feel a transference of purpose and power and fight. It was as if the photo called to me. To look at it again, to really see. There is a warped strip of old Scotch tape residue on the photo. I'm afraid to play around with it, for fear of tearing the fragile old paper and losing the young couple forever. Also, I like its presence; it signifies this is a photo that had once been cherished and displayed for all to see. The best of the batch, the one that makes you say, "Aww, look. That's a keeper." Had it been fixed above my father's glove box? Taped on the refrigerator, maybe? Stuck to Grandpa Jesperson's nineteenth-century rolltop desk?

The young Pacific coast couple in this photo is giddy and wear smiles that stretch every muscle in their faces. Behind the couple lies a harvested field of what is likely alfalfa on Grandpa Jesperson's farm, tucked in the lower valley of Yakima, Washington. Whoever snapped this shot most definitely had their back to the crest of the Cascade Range.

The photo is time-stamped August 1978, eleven months before I was born. Surely my mother and father are working on bringing me into the world. I decide it's their anniversary, their first as married people, and I imagine Grandpa Les, with his camera strapped around his neck, saying something like, "Come on, lovebirds, smile for the camera. Go on, Keith, pretend you like this woman." It is clear from my dad's expression that he truly did.

I study my mother, so impossibly young here in this photo, and remember something else she said while in hospice. "The first years of our marriage were so much fun," she said. They traveled around and experienced new places. She joined a new family, leaving her childhood of poverty and abandonment behind. This new world "opened up in ways I never knew before," she said in a wondering tone of voice. My dad gave my mom that wonder. He gave my mom me.

This was the first time I thought of my father as having given anything. Dad is the one who took—people, lives, futures, hope. The young man in this old photo is not the Happy Face Killer. This man, whose mammoth six-foot-six body embraces my mother protectively, is Keith. Just Keith. A young guy in love.

Having a killer in the family is like a dried-up piece of tape over a treasured photograph, that if peeled off leaves a blemish where something used to be; and over time, you forget anything good had existed in the first place. So much of my work requires me to help others examine their lives after discovering that they have a killer in their family. The irony is that a lot of that reflection is dependent on recalling life before there was a killer in the family. Pieces of the memories have been violently torn away, leaving blemishes in their place, but underneath those torn-away spots is the vanished reality of what once was.

I study the photo once again. My mom's spunky smile lifts her chin up. I feel happy to see her again and sad because she exudes the faith and hope and pride I rarely saw in my lifetime. It's the only picture I have that shows her to be happy in the way I want to remember her. It's bizarre to realize that Keith standing next to her is who gave her that joy—I wouldn't believe it if I didn't have this picture to prove it. Never mind the blemishes that mar the photo, never mind the blemishes that mar my memories; I was born from my parents' happiness. At the genesis there was love.

And love is what I want to bring to my future.

ACKNOWLEDGMENTS

MELISSA G. MOORE

For my mother, Rose, who kept the light on when everything went dark. Though she's no longer here, I think of her every time a light flickers—it always brings me back to her story of fireflies, tiny sparks of hope in the darkest fields. Her light is reflected in these pages.

To my literary agent, Marilyn Allen. Thank you for believing in this story long before it had shape or certainty. You are equal parts compass and calm, and I'm endlessly grateful to have you on this journey.

To my coauthor, Michele, for five years, this book was our constant companion. Through loss and love, through moves and remodels, through the chaos of real life, we kept returning to it. We wrote in hotel rooms and airports, across time zones and holidays, refusing to stop until the story finally spoke for itself.

To my husband, Steve Kenoyer, and our five children, Aspen, Jake, Natalie, Cody, and River—thank you for your patience as my time and attention were often devoted to this book.

To Julie McCarron, who cheered us on in our darkest hour and pushed us to believe again in this project after a few setbacks—with a capital *T* for tenacity. Wink, wink. Your faith and friendship reignited our hope when we needed it most.

Thank you to the BenBella team for your trust, guidance, and for making this book a reality.

MICHELE MATRISCIANI

The journey of this book began more than five years ago with a phone call from Melissa G. Moore, inviting me into what she called her life's work. *Killer in the Family* began as a spark of an idea and grew into an ambition that captured both Melissa's heart and mine. I'm grateful it did. Melissa, you have an instinct for illuminating what others overlook and a fearless commitment to exploring the complexities of humanity. Thank you for trusting me (again) with your work and for making this one of the most rewarding—and challenging—projects of my career. I will forever be an enthusiastic passenger on the "Melissa Train."

To our literary agent, Marilyn Allen, for joining us on another publishing adventure. For five years, you helped us navigate the unexpected, hear out our ideas (and choice words!), and showed us how to professionally and gracefully embrace the art of the pivot, including fitting two other books into the mix. We are fortunate to have a publishing great like you by our side!

BenBella Books has been a remarkable place to call our publishing home. Thank you to publisher Glenn Yeffeth for believing in us and in this book and for providing the talented champion and editor, Rick Chillot. BIG shoutout to Scott Calamar, whose developmental editing supported the voices of every family member involved and made the process so much fun that I felt guilty calling it work. Congratulations on your retirement, Scott! I'm so glad we were able to be part of your swan song.

To my friends and family, for cheering on both Melissa and me and not losing steam over the last five years. Thank you to Carol Rosenberg for her early editing assistance and friendship.

Matthew, Daniel, and Julian, my three men who supportively send me hand signals (mostly for food) through the panes of my office door, thank you for your focus on helping me stay focused. You are my life.

Finally, this book would not be in its current form without the talented writer Julie McCarron, who has always been in my corner, personally and professionally. Her editorial guidance, insight, and unwavering support helped us navigate challenges, break through editorial walls, and bring this project to life.

L: Michele; R: Melissa
Julie Shuford Photography

ABOUT THE AUTHORS

Melissa G. Moore is a *New York Times* bestselling author and Emmy-nominated filmmaker known for her fearless storytelling and pursuit of truth. The daughter of serial killer Keith Jesperson—infamously known as the "Happy Face Killer"—Melissa has dedicated her career to exposing the hidden toll of violence and exploring how survivors rebuild their lives in its aftermath.

Her work has been featured in *Forbes*, *TIME*, and *People*, and inspired the Paramount+ series *Happy Face*. Through her books, documentaries, and films, Melissa continues to illuminate the dark corners of human experience with empathy, insight, and unflinching honesty. She lives between Oregon and Sicily with her husband, Steve.

Michele Matrisciani is a *New York Times* bestselling author and editor. As the founder of Bookchic LLC, she works with authors to turn ideas into books that captivate readers and make an impact. An MFA graduate from Stony Brook University and a Pushcart Prize nominee, Michele blends creativity, insight, and editorial expertise to guide writers from inspiration to publication. Discover more at michelem.net.